Crop Circles, Gods and their Secrets

Frontier Publishing

Adventures Unlimited Press

Crop Circles, Gods and their Secrets

Robert J. Boerman

Frontier Publishing
Adventures Unlimited Press

First Print: 2000
Second print: 2004

Published by Frontier Publishing
P.O. Box 48
1600 AA Enkhuizen
the Netherlands
Tel: +31-(0)228-324076
Fax: +31-(0)228-312081
E-mail: fp@fsf.nl
Website: www.fsf.nl

© Robert J. Boerman 2000
Translated by Marijke Bouma
Book and cover design: Robert J. Boerman
Cover photographs: © Janet Ossebaard
ISBN 1-931882-25-8

Contents

Chapter 3
The origin of the Great Pyramid

Chapter 4
Return of the gods

Chapter 5
The crop circle makers reveal themselves

Preface

'Boerman you will write a book someday!' These words spoken by a Dutch crop circle researcher still echo in my ears. He had said this when I had delivered a few articles concerning the crop circle phenomenon for his website. *'Not me, that's not for me'*, was my reply to him, but he was already the third person who had said something like that to me. That sure makes you think and gives you something of a writers itch. Never had I ever contemplated the idea of writing a book. It was always something that seemed extremely difficult and something done by 'other' people. The idea to write a book about my own discoveries regarding the mysterious crop circles remained however and wouldn't leave my thoughts.

From the moment that I first came in touch with the crop circle phenomenon I have had a very strong feeling that there were messages hidden in various crop circles that could be deciphered. Only the big question was; how would you go about doing that. After a course of time and much philosophising I started with the inscription that was found in 1991 close to Alton Barnes. This formation has always fascinated me; more so because from the time of introduction to this formation I had an increased feeling that there was much more to this formation then that which could be seen at face value. When I finally succeeded in reading this formation I was amazed about the information that this inscription had concealed within it.

Later on I just 'happened' to come into contact with a few people that could help me more. With the joint effort of these people I ultimately succeeded in combining all the information that was available to me concerning the facts on how to be able to create a system that could decode crop circles. One of these people is Hellen Venix, who has her practice in Kinesiology, which she also combines with her gift as a medium. I ended up at her office after a bout with tennis elbow. Hellen told me that she could probably alleviate the pain from the tennis elbow and sure enough after the second treatment the pain had gotten much better. During her treatments she asked me what I was doing to stay busy and I told her that I was writing a book about crop circles. I told her a few things I knew for a fact, and I also mentioned a few things about which I had my doubts. Hellen kept on telling me over and over; 'yes, that's right,… that is also right,…and this is how it is and so on'. To my complete astonishment she didn't have a clue as to what she was talking about but she did know all the answers I needed! When I questioned her as to how she knew all these things she informed me she had 'been given' this information fourteen days ago. Now I'm definitely not one of those people that accepts everything without thinking; but further experience with her 'messages' have convinced me that these 'pieces of information' were correct. All the facts that were traceable I made an effort to track down and the striking thing is that the facts are exactly as she described them to me.

I also picked up a bunch of stuff from Hylke Welling. He has kept himself occupied with research into Atlantis and Egypt for more than thirty years thereby collecting a treasure chest full of valuable information. Amongst this pot of gold there is information available that you never hear about anymore these days. This is something that is very strange because this information that is accessible to us could contribute to re-writing the history of mankind. The drawback to that would be that the various disciplines of the sciences that have been involved with this for many years would have to adjust their proclaimed opinions. As far as ancient Egypt is concerned Welling is like a walking encyclopaedia and he is the one who set me on the right track of the ancient Arab writings that date the Great Pyramid of Giza at a much different time from that generally accepted.

I am also very thankful to Ora van Oostende who, because of her knowledge of the Hebrew language, was able to help me enormously with the deciphering of, amongst other things, the inscription at Alton Barnes. Without her I would never have been able to 'read' crop circles.

Evert Poorterman was the person who told me several years ago about the books of Zecharia Sitchin. Since then we have discussed for many, many hours about almost any historical subject and our interpretation of the history of mankind.

And at last but not at least, I would like to thank Marijke Bouma who did an enormous job translating this book. Without her help I wouldn't have been able to publish this book in the English language.

Furthermore I want to thank Henk Groenewoud, Dees Wilson, Peter Toonen, Bert Janssen, Janet Ossebaard, Hans Rijpstra, Pepe Vrolijk, Marianne Ringelberg, Pieter van de Poll, George Bishop CCCS UK (Centre for Crop Circle Studies), Andreas Müller of the ICCA (the International Crop Circle Archive), Zecharia Sitchin, Gerald Hawkins, Michael Green CCCS UK, Andrew King, Lucy Pringle, Colin Andrews, Alan Alford for their contributions to this book by means of ideas, tips or pictures. Without the help of all these people this book would have never come to fruition.

Thank you all.

Robert Boerman, Brummen, the Netherlands 2003

Introduction

Ever since the early days of my childhood I have been interested in everyday and unusual things. On my eleventh birthday I received a gigantic Winkler-Prins family atlas. A splendid book that I fortunately still own today. Once in a while I still look at it and as usual my attention is drawn to the first colour photograph that is encountered in it. It is a picture of our Earth, taken from behind the Moon. Beside it are quoted the first lines of Genesis, which together with the next ten verses were read by the crew of the American spaceship, Apollo 8, during the historical flight around the Moon in 1968. In this picture the Earth is embedded in the eternal blackness of our immeasurable universe. I found it to be such a fascinating picture that I often asked myself what was beyond the infinite blackness and what was our place in this boundless universe.

More than a year later on July 16, 1969, at 09:32 Eastern Standard Time, the majestic Apollo 11 was launched from platform 39-A at Cape Kennedy. When Armstrong became the first human to ever-set foot on the Moon I was six years old. To this day I can still remember the excitement of the people around me. It was quite something, the thought of a man on the Moon almost inconceivable especially for a six year old. I was already fascinated even then by that white orb that showed a different phase each night in the heavens.

I received the above-mentioned atlas, which described the Milky Way, stars and planets with their distances from us, several years after the first landing on the Moon. Even then I was already asking myself how could it be possible that only one planet in the solar system had sustainable life on it. There were at least eight planets besides ours: Could we possibly be the only ones in this unfathomable, astronomical universe? All these questions kept resurfacing at a later time in my life. The older you get the more questions cross your path. You roll from one interesting subject into another without ever getting an answer to the proposed questions. And then comes the time when you are submerged so deeply into an answer that there is no way back and you literally become infected with the answers. Something that has kept you occupied at the level of a hobby now becomes so important it encompasses your daily life.

It happened to me at a crop circle formation seminar given by a Dutch crop circleresearcher Rudi Klijnstra in February 1997. Due to Rudi's involvement in research on crop circles over many years he had become very knowledgeable on this subject matter. With immense pleasure I attentively followed his lecture that evening and much to my liking ended up in a conversation with him afterwards. I told him that I was under the assumption that throughout the world, in various grain fields, messages have been written over the years that we do not understand as of yet but that they are received by our subconscious. At the end of our conversation Rudi asked me if I would call him if there was ever anything special to see in our region as far as crop circles were concerned. Of course I was willing to do just that and after a moment of thought I told him I was convinced that something extraordinary was to happen that year and I would be calling him. Don't ask me how it's possible but I just knew that I would be phoning him.

Months later as I was watching the starry heavens, keeping my eye out for falling stars I had long forgotten my pronouncement to Rudi. Before I turned in for the night I threw a question into the sky and asked if I could see something beautiful before crawling under the blankets. With barely a wink my wishes were granted, after a second the most ethereal 'falling star' appeared. It was so beautiful and clear that it took my breath away. Not knowing what was awaiting me the next day, this had been a perfect ending to an evening of stargazing.

The next day my family and I spent the rest of our holiday funds as we took a round trip by plane from the airport in Teuge. We were barely in the air when I casually asked the pilot if he had ever seen a crop circle formation. He told us he had not but mainly because the subject matter did not interest him and he had never bothered looking.

Within ten minutes the pilot pointed to something unusual. I looked in the direction at which he pointed and almost went through the roof of the small Cessna plane. A genuine crop circle formation five miles as the crow flies from my home! This flight resulted in the first documented discovery of the crop circle pictogram of Brummen in 1997.

Once we had landed safely on the ground I went to have a closer look at the pictogram. Disappointingly enough once I approached the pictogram on the ground I discovered it to be two or three weeks old already. The grain around it had already started to recuperate and return to its original vertical position.

This shows us that you really don't have to go out looking but these things just happen to you when the time is right. It automatically happens especially when you open your mind to allow these things to enter it. All this sounds very familiar to some people and they will continue throughout the years with their methods of research. Each one of us holds a small piece of the truth and hopefully one day the time will come when all the pieces of the puzzle will come together and give us the one and final truth.

Crop Circles, Gods and their Secrets

1

Crop circles: a historical and contemporary phenomenon

Crop circles, works of Man?

In general people consider you to be pretty crazy and an airhead when they discover that something so intangible as crop circles is what keeps you occupied. Helicopters and thicket mowers! These are all terms and accusations that are whispered under people's breath when you let them know the subject of crop circles greatly interests you. 'You don't believe all that nonsense do you? Last week on the Discovery Channel they were still showing that it is all the works of man. Wasn't it proven that it is all the handy work of two pensioners, Doug and Dave, who created all these formations'? But could that possibly be the truth? Are we to assume that all these years we have been fooled by two senior citizens that jump from country to country? Or are there people engaged in crop circle artistry all over the world creating replicas of crop circle formations just to make fools out of the rest of the population? Is that possible for more than a decade? Come on people, wake up! Do you really believe that mankind has created all the more than 10,000 recorded crop circle formations? What about all the unrecorded formations? Obviously it is a waste of your time and frustrating if you have been up all night duplicating a crop circle formation and not a soul discovers your creation. Naturally the best thing that could happen is that someone discovers your reproduction and that preferably you get all the media coverage possible. The best part is that with a straight face you get to tell the world that it was really all your own doing.

Crop circles, a creation of the last few years?

Are all the crop circles that have been recorded since the 1970s only from the last three decades? Most people believe that this phenomenon is indeed something from the past twenty or thirty years but actually that is far from reality. There is a report that dates back to 1633. When a Mr. Hart was walking around in the middle of the night in Wiltshire, England he came upon 'green circles' with' innumerable quantities of pygmies or a miniature folk who danced around and around'. Mr. Hart further proceeded to share with the world that he was continually being 'pinched' by these peoples as they produced a humming sound. The most famous example that we know of. dates back to a pamphlet written in 1678 in Hartfortshire, England in which a 'Mowing Devil' is mentioned as the culprit who 'reaped' a crop circle formation. The impressed landlord of the property was deeply moved by how the devil was able to in one night to place each and every stalk precisely in such a way that whomever tried to duplicate this formation would be occupied for the rest of their lives. In the Old French manuscript 'Le Grandine' dated back to 815 AD the Bishop of Lyon is warning his new curate by letter, of the strange practices of his new parishioners: this is because of the strange illustrations in the crops that were described as works of the Devil. The locals were reputed to trade crop from their afflicted fields with alien aerial visitors and traffic with weather magicians. Many choose to see this as proof of crop circle activity. In even older documented writings, specifically speaking of the 12,000-year-old Sanskrit texts; it seems that even then one talked of crop circle formations. Therefore one can figure out that it is not something of the last two decades but that these formations have been present forever. The next event also points to the above-mentioned fact. When a farmer near Wiltshire was told that there was a crop circle formation on his property his reaction was that he wasn't surprised because it was something his father had already showed him as a small boy. As long as the man could remember in the last 28 years there had been annual crop circles in his field.

Crop circle pioneers

It is well known that since the early seventies crop circles occur regularly in England. Earlier reports are not generally very well known except for the few mentioned earlier. Colin Andrews, Busty Taylor and Pat Delgado are the true crop circle pioneers. They started their research in the early eighties. In the beginning the formations were simple clockwise turning circles but from 1987 onwards the circles occasionally became counter-clock wise formations. The patterns in the circles varied from very simple flat unbroken stalks to very complicated patterns where the stalks had been placed over and under each other. There were also circles found where the crops in the middle pointed to the outside. Over the years the circles have evolved to be magnificent pictograms (see illustrations).

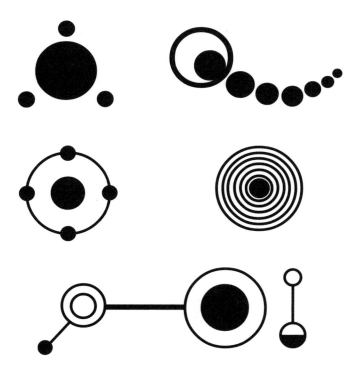

In 1989 the total number of discovered and recorded crop circles had almost reached 100 and in the next year more than 300 were discovered. Over of the last few years crop circles have been encountered all over the world. Professor Peshotan Mehta is the person who occupies himself with this subject matter in India. Amongst other things a triangle has been found with a 'Star of David' in it. This was discovered in a wheat field and it had a 420metre diameter with the star having a 250 meter diameter. A complicated illustration of an hourglass accompanied by two circles on each of its narrower sides with two small circles inside those has also been found. This formation had an enormous measurement of 1000 metres in total length. Professor Mehta tells us that crop circles have been appearing in India for thousands of years. He saw 'his' first formation on Christmas Eve of 1965 (see illustrations).

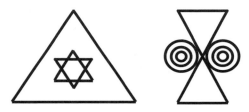

A radar picture made on January 4th, 1999 west of New York City, USA even depicts a cloud circle formation. Experts attribute this to a mistake made in the installation of one or more of the radar towers. I did some further research and it is possible that one or more radar transmitters can interfere with each other and therefore this strange pattern can appear (see illustration).

Research to ... deceptive information?

In 1990 Colin Andrews and Pat Delgado set up an extensive crop circle research campaign. This was mainly due to the fact that the Ministers of Defence, Agriculture and Environment had actually met to discuss this 'new' phenomenon. So the two gentlemen decided to pursue the manner on a much larger scale. Of course the news media was very intrigued by this. The BBC and NipponTV were the main sponsors for this research event that had been set up by Andrews and Delgado. The BBC and NipponTV made a large contribution to this event by donating infrared cameras. After the Ministers had met two military men, who wanted to assist with the research, approached Mr. Andrews. Mr. Andrews refused their partnership.

From the observation post on the morning of July 25th, 1990 it seemed as if a crop circle formation had been created in the distance. After a few enthusiastic comments made by Mr. Andrews in front of the camera it wasn't long before he had to take back his short-lived excitement as inspection quickly proved that it was a hoax. Researchers now generally think that military authorities were responsible for these replicas especially since just beyond the reach of the infrared cameras a wooden cross and horoscope discs were placed in the centre of the circle. Later on Doug and Dave appeared out of nowhere and said they were responsible for all the crop circles. There are also rumours going around that there are more bodies/entities who are responsible for some hoax formations. But why would one do this? One possibility that comes to mind is that those responsible for the hoax formations know more then we think they know. What do you do then? Exactly, you take care that everyone thinks that man has formulated all the crop circles in order to prevent uncomfortable questions, havoc and unnecessary research. Isn't that what happened in Roswell in 1947? It is very obvious that something crashed but up until today it is not clear as to what happened there. If in fact one turns to falsification and deceptive information of say for example the crop circles then the average citizen attributes the crop circles to jokers who keep themselves occupied through wind and weather in all hours of the night to create these crop circles with the help of a piece of wood and a rope.

According to George Wingfield, a former member of the British CCCS it was decided that after a meeting of various British Ministers, that the British Ministry of Defence would take appropriate measures, including deceptive information to reduce the excitement amongst the general public.

When I discovered the pictogram in Brummen, the Netherlands, it didn't take long before it was rumoured that I was responsible for the formation. Unfortunately it did appear at rather an inconvenient time. It was just after a few of us had established a foundation for those who were interested in paranormal and unusual occurrences. The first lecture took place on September 11, 1997. Eltjo Haselhoff, a Dutch scientist, who certainly dares to describe crop circles in a scientific manner, would bear the brunt of the battle with his lecture on crop circles.

A few days after the discovery of the pictogram in Brummen there was a picture of it in our regional newspaper. Due to the media coverage the public automatically presumed it to be a publicity stunt on our behalf. Truly we had nothing to do with the formation and Dr. Levengood proved this. Dr. Levengood and his BLT team showed us that the sticky white substance could not be duplicated without it costing millions of dollars. At that point he was not even referring to all the apparatus needed to reproduce this material.

In any case, there are now more than 10.000 recorded crop circle formations. Could they all be men made? If you consider that in 1997 in Zierikzee (the Netherlands) the creators of the hoax (see photograph next page) spent more than 300 hundred man hours with the preparations and two nights of fieldwork, then it is amazing that there are still people out there who claim that there are formations many times bigger than the one found in Zierikzee which are made in a much shorter time span than the one that the Zeeuwse gentlemen were able to accomplish.

What does science says?

The first time I heard of a crop circle was in 1996. I had heard about an aerial photograph of a crop circle formation just outside of Zutphen (the Netherlands). It had caught my attention before but I was not aware of the finer details of this phenomenon. A few days later I thought I should go have a look and see what all the fuss was about but unfortunately there was nothing left to see. It seemed that the property owner was afraid that too many people would come onto his land and destroy the rest of his crop so he took matters into his own hands and harvested the remaining crop.

Once back home you start to ask yourself what could possibly bring about a crop circle formation. Many different theories have been cited throughout the years but none of these are very conclusive. The question remains as to who or what did this and why? There is hardly a learned scholar who wants to get burned on the subject matter of crop circles because in general they have been written off as nonsense and the work of man. The crop circles have also been associated with UFO's. So who wants to be associated with UFO's, crop circles and more of this celestial nonsense? No one! Fortunately there are people who keep themselves occupied with this because it is extremely intriguing material. The more you get to know about this subject, the more questions arise which causes you to look for more answers and explanations and so the story can start over again from the beginning.

As far as scientific research is concerned, there simply isn't very much due to the fact that there is hardly a scholar around who wants to be declared a nutcase by his colleagues when he tells them that in his spare time he studies crop circle formations. Fortunately there are the odd scientists who seriously want to know what it is all about and are very dedicated to the cause. One of those people is Dr. William Levengood, an American Bio-Physicist, who in collaboration with the BLT team (that's not bacon, lettuce and tomato! but John **B**urke, William **L**evengood and Nancy **T**albot) has been analysing plant and soil samples that have been sent to him from all over world since 1989. He researched samples that were taken from within the circles compared to those, which were found outside of the circles so that he would have some comparison material. He noticed a few remarkable things such as; that on some seedheads that looked normal on the outside, not a single seed was left in them. He also noted that under identical growing circumstances at the laboratories the samples of seeds from the inside of the circles grew faster than those taken from the outside of the circle. There have been spectacular discoveries by Dr. Levengood in the Netherlands due to rare findings there. The white crystal powder, which was found at the site of the 1996 pictogram outside of Zutphen, arises from a natural friction temperature of more than 3000 degrees Celsius and it is of unknown origin. The white, sticky substance (see photograph next page) that I found myself in the pictogram in Brummen in 1997 has been tested. It is a silicone-hydrogen compound that is so pure that it is actually too expensive to make. I also took a sample of this white stuff to be tested through means of Kinesiology (the study of the mechanics of human movement) to discover that the material allowed you to 'ground' better and that there was better contact with 'up above'. Your vibrations are literally increased. The average rate at which someone feels very fit is a value of approximately 3,600. When the white substance was tested on myself I had a value of

6,500 and believe me I felt fit as a fiddle! I carry an aura protector with me and when I put that away and was re-tested my value shot up to 10,000. After a few months it was tested again and it had increased to 18,000! That means that I felt 5x more wonderful than the average person who is feeling great at 3600. I had the feeling that my value increased too quickly so I put the material away for a while because I could not keep up to it.

Around the whole world only a few similar findings have ever been recorded. A few of which were discovered at UFO landing sites in countries such as Russia, the United States and Israel. Most of the time we are speaking of very small amounts but at the site in Brummen there was so much of the white substance you could literally scoop it up. Outside of the scientific studies, also being done by Dr. Eltjo Haselhoff, there are various people occupied with discovering the secrets of the crop circle formations.

Answer from Orion?

Hans-Jurgen Kyborg and Joachim Koch, two German amateur astronomers who have kept themselves occupied with crop circle research since 1989, have researched various English crop circles. From their experience they think they have the solution to the crop circle formations. The two researchers have discovered the code of the crop circles by looking at the hieroglyphics in an ancient Egyptian family burial vault.

By means of self made crop circles, which are an answer to the crop circles from the year before, the two amateur astronomers believe that they have made contact with the 'makers' of the crop circles. They presume that the beings of Orion are involved with the crop circle phenomenon and that the formations contain astronomical information. They use the crop circles as a communication method between themselves and the 'crop circle makers'.

All of this is truly a possibility but unfortunately it does not jive for all of the crop circles because basically that would mean that all the mysteries around the crop circles would be solved and then there wouldn't be any more questions any more. Instead the questions become more numerous as time goes on. The more we talk about it the more questions arise. Several crop circle formation experts including the Hopi Indians and the Tibetan Lamas claim that they are a signal from Mother Earth herself. According to them this phenomenon can actually take place because the Earth creates energy and an interaction occurs with 'something' in the cosmos. It could be an interaction because a lot of the crop circles have been found on the leylines. So what exactly are leylines, and what is that 'something' in the cosmos?

Leylines

In 1846 there was a book published by clergyman Edward Duke. The book was called 'The Druidical Temples of Wilts'. It was a study carried out by Duke into the ancient monuments in the county of Wiltshire. He came to the conclusion that Celtic priests, the Druids, were responsible for the prehistoric constructions. Duke discovered a remarkable north-south line on which several prehistoric monuments were built.

At William Henry Black's presentation on the 6th of September, 1870 he told his audience that in his twenty years as a researcher of secret lines in among such places as India, China, Europe, there were a striking amount of old monuments that were situated on these lines. It wasn't his night, however, and the general public declared him to be slightly deranged. He continued with his research but passed away 2 years later. Many others followed Duke and Black with the research on the leylines. It actually took until 1982 for the leylines to be scientifically acknowledged.

Leylines are lines in the landscapes. They are not visible but with the help of a divining rod, pendulum or bare hands they can be found. It does require experience with the above-mentioned means. Quite often these straight lines connect old churches, castles and monasteries with each other. On these lines one also finds burial mounds, menhirs and stone circles of which Stonehenge is the most famous. Leylines run in different layers above and beneath the Earth. They are not real energy lines but where the leylines cross this is known as the leycentre. At the point of the leycentre there is a very strong energy level, which is noticeable and measurable. These lines are found all over the world and amongst many other places they connect the pyramids of Giza, the Nazca plateau, Stonehenge and the Bermuda triangle with each other.

Some writers think that shamans used the Nazca lines to take a soul trip along these lines into the astral world. Russian research has proven that leylines can be used to send signals. Professor Alexander Trefimov has performed research on leylines and telepathy. The discoveries were striking. In a cave with high magnetic value that was situated on a crossing of leylines, various messages were 'signalled' to Novosibirsk, in Bulgary, thousands of kilometres away. Days later the messages were still being received. This was attributed to the strong energy transfers. This same experiment was tried from a regular cave without the magnetic value and not a single signal came in.

Dutch crop circles

The Netherlands has been participating quite nicely in crop circles over the last few years. It all started here in 1986. From that year comes the first mention of a crop circle formation that was found in Usselo (Enschede). In the first nine years of the discoveries only 47 crop circles were recorded. From then on discoveries became more numerous but not as much as in England. Along with the mention of a crop circle in Usselo came the mention of a circle in the ice in Usselo. The ice was so thin that there was no way anyone could have walked on it. The big bang came in 1996 when 97 discoveries were mentioned and recorded. A striking discovery was the pictogram in the snow on December 31st, 1996. The pictogram appeared during the night of the 30th into the 31st of December on a snowy field. There wasn't a single footstep to be found.

The original numbers of findings are higher but not all the crop circles have been made public therefore they could not be recorded nor investigated. In 1997 there were only fifty a somewhat meagre year compared to the record of 1996. 1998 was an extremely pitiful year as far as reported incidents were concerned. Barely a dozen reports came into the crop circle reporting station.

Even though there weren't very many incidents reported in 1998 it was still a very interesting year. Besides the regular reports of grass and grain circles there was a different phenomenon to admire this year. This was namely the 'cut off' corn. The first report of this came in on May 25th, 1998 at the Lattrop National Observatory. Someone had discovered a very unique finding in a field of immature corn plants of approximately 25cm high. It looked like an odd 'tractor track' but upon closer consideration of the 'track' one could see that there was absolutely no evidence of foot or tyre prints on the land. The total length of this pattern was 86 metres.

The second reporting of the 'cut off corn' came on the 28th of May. The length of this corn pictogram was an astounding 300 metres! A new Dutch record was set. This pictogram was situated 3 kilometres away from the previous finding in the cornfield in Rossum. In this cornfield the corn was also 'cut' just as in the previous discovery. On one side of this pictogram one finds a grass circle.

On the 6th of August of that same year I was the discoverer of the third cereal pictogram. I was cycling around in the neighbourhood and at a distance of no more than 500 metres from my own home I saw something strange in the cornfield. My eye immediately fell upon some 'cut off' cereal stalks. Initially your reaction is to think it is some sort of practical joke. It looked like someone had taken a chopping knife or something similar to that and had cut off a few rows of corn. But after I looked around carefully there really weren't any human or tyre tracks to be seen. Immediately I thought about the pictograms in Rossum. The crop from the first 6 rows was 'cut off' thick and the plants that were 'cut-off' varied from the 1st to the 6th row from fourteen to five pieces (stalks). The height at which the cereal had been 'cut off' was at about 1.20 metres. Look carefully at the close-up picture of the crop where it shows that the crop just keeps on growing.

The most striking element of this pictogram was that the three farthest to the right crop stalks had been cut twice; therefore creating two pieces that lay beside it. All the others had only been cut once. In one of the twice-cut pieces there was even a small cut in the middle of that. The total height of the 'cut-off' crop was approximately 1.20 metres. The stumps of the remaining plants were an average of 30 – 50 cms. During the discovery it was noted that the crop was almost mature which meant that the pictogram was already three weeks old. When we checked with the owner of the property he confirmed that at approx. three weeks prior he had noticed an odd design in his field but had chalked it up to teenage pranks. The wondrous thing is that over the last three years of all the pictograms found close to Brummen they all lay along the railway line Arnhem/Zutphen. The pictogram found in Zutphen in 1996 (which is actually territory that belongs to Brummen) lies at the same distance from the railway line as the pictogram found in Brummen, namely at 500 metres from railway line Arnhem/Zutphen. The cornfield is actually also located

750 metres from the tracks. Could it be possible that railway lines and electricity pylons are a sort of 'leyline' used by the 'crop circle makers' to create their 'messages'? Or are 'they' using the railroad tracks and leylines as a navigational guide as to where to place the formations?

Crop circles, leylines and holy places

Many crop circles have been found in the neighbourhoods of old relics and sanctuaries such as Stonehenge, Avebury and Silbury Hill. Many of those formations were found to be on leylines. Having become curious as to whether this was so as far as our formations were concerned I contacted Arie van Bodegom who belongs to the Archaeology Society of Brummen. Arie was able to share with me that in earlier days on the Kanonsdike in Zutphen, where the Zutphen pictogram of 1996 was discovered, there used to be an old castle. In the 1920's there were prehistoric burial mounds discovered at the site of the 1997 pictogram discovery in Brummen. These burial mounds were destroyed by being dug up and used to level off roads in the area. The 'cut off' crop discovery in Oeken (regional district of Brummen) was only a stones throw away from an old chapel that stood there until approximately the end of the 1700s. Together with Arie van Bodegom I made up a very precise map of the surrounding areas of where the three pictograms were discovered and we came to the conclusion that all three discoveries were situated on the same leyline. The line of the crop pictograms actually goes right through my living room! All these formations are situated on the same leyline and all three of them close to an old sanctuary.

Only corn?

Besides the unique crop formations there were also other crop circles to admire. The most exquisite one is the finding in August 1998. It was the second formation of Hypolitushoef because earlier on in the same year there had been the first discovery on the 17th of June.

There were also some formations reported in Slenaken and Oud-beijerland. This helped to make 1998 a somewhat worthwhile crop circle year (see illustrations).

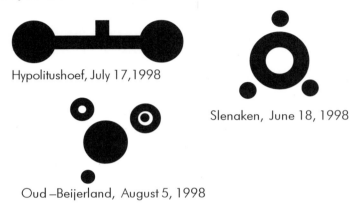

Hypolitushoef, July 17,1998

Slenaken, June 18, 1998

Oud –Beijerland, August 5, 1998

Dutch hoax formations

Of course there were some hoax formations made in 1998. By hoax I mean that these formations have been created by man. Man's handiwork was present at the crop circle that was discovered on the 17th of August close to Markelo (Province of Overijssel) by Ben Wolf during a balloon flight. The owner had given permission three weeks previous to make a crop circle formation to be present during the town's annual festivities. The plan was get the media involved on that day and to unravel the 'mystery' of the crop circle during the celebrations. Unfortunately the press excused themselves and the creators of the crop circle never got the publicity that they were hoping for.

The Society of Awake Animals was actually able to achieve a formation in the form of a pig that had a diameter of 70 metres in the grain fields in the neighbourhood of Assen (Province of Drenthe). It had been created in protest against the then still not solved problems of the health and welfare of pigs in the Netherlands. What the Society of Awake Animals wanted to accomplish with this feat was to ensure that pigs would have their housing on straw and not on concrete gratings (see photograph).

During one of my first flights in 1998 we were flying above Gorssel (Province of Gelderland). We had barely been in the plane for ten minutes when out of the corner of my eye I spotted a green pasture down below which had been turned yellow by the many dandelions that were present. Inside this area were four green circles. My curiosity had been aroused and we landed near the above-mentioned pasture. After some close fieldwork I made some enquiries at nearby farms. A kind, horse back riding young lady gave me an answer to my question. A bit confused by the answer I left the area but just checked one more time at another neighbours for confirmation on this particular answer given to me by the young lady. The neighbour confirmed that there had been a neighbourhood party a few days ago and that on the schedule of events for the party there was a golf tournament. For the golf tournament four circles of grass had been mowed in the pasture otherwise one could not play golf in the high grass! So yes, man had made indeed the grass circles, there was simply no other cause but it did look odd from in the sky!

1998 was a meagre year but it was different!

All in all 1998 was a meagre year and one tends to wonder how could this be all of a sudden? There is, as yet, no logical explanation to be found for this. During a conversation with Rudi Klijnstra he shared with me the fact that he was having a conversation with Mark Fussel of the Internet Crop Circle Connector in England this summer. He was able to state a reason for the drastic decline of crop circles in the Netherlands. One of the reasons could be that after the discovery of the first big hoax formation in Zierikzee in 1997 the real 'makers' could have received such a shock they are now hesitant to return. It is as if the hoax in Zierikzee takes and is negative while the three-sided Julia spiral is the opposite. This one gives and is positive (see photographs next page). I will write more about the possible conse-quences of hoax in the next chapter.

We will probably never discover as to why there were less discoveries in 1998 than in previous years but it is a possibility that the 'circle-makers' of the formations want us to focus our attention on other things now, whatever those 'things' might be.

Geometry in crop circles

One of the things we should probably pay more attention to is the geometry found within various different formations.. Most of the formations cannot be produced without accompanying detailed calculations. There are formations that we know of that appears to be very clear in that if there were people who wanted to reproduce the particular formation that they would have to place the construction lines outside the formations. Precise work is also required especially considering that the smallest mistake has large consequences for the rest of the formation. One centimeter too far to the left or right can make all the different in the world and throw off the whole formation yet to be completed.

At a first glance it appears that various crop circles have just been

Zierikzee, July 17, 1997

Windmill Hill, August 2, 1996

made in the field. It doesn't seem as if they have been placed according to a pattern but first appearances can be deceptive. There really is some sort of geometrical relationship within the formations. Bert Janssen is one of the people who occupies himself with geometry in crop circles. During the time that he still lived in Groningen an associate regularly informed him of matters that went farther than any of the accepted facts accepted by science thus far. Information about UFOs and crop circles. Bert wasn't interested in the crop circle phenomenon, until he came home from a holiday in the early 90s when there was an enormous pile of mail and newspapers lying on his doormat.

Bert told me that "In one of those newspapers there was an photograph of a crop circle, close to Assen. That was so close to Groningen that I thought, this I have to see. The only thing the newspaper stated was that it was situated to the south of Assen. I quickly jumped in the car and headed towards Assen where I spent the whole day looking for that formation. After I had almost given up all hope of finding the crop circle, I came around a corner and suddenly I saw it lying there. The strange thing was that the newspaper had mentioned a very large circle but this one was relatively small with 4 small circles surrounding it. After I looked around for a bit I walked to the car to call my girlfriend, but halfway there I turned around and something caught my eye. I couldn't see the circles. Even when I was at the car I couldn't see them, while I was absolute positive that I had seen them from the car. You couldn't see them from the road, but yet I had seen them. Later on I discovered that there were 'merely' two formations close to Assen and the chance that you would just walk upon one in a field is extremely small. It was too insane for words. How was it possible that I was absolutely positive that I had seen the circles from the road, while you couldn't see them from that point? The whole event moved me so much from that moment on I thought 'Now I'm first going to England to see if this is a serious phenomenon or if it is all nonsense'."

From one thing comes another and that is how Janssen came in touch with the geometry in crop circles. If you examine the

Crop Circles, Gods and their Secrets

formations worked out by him, then it is hard to imagine (almost impossible) what is involved in how a certain formation is constructed. It is even the case, that if a certain line or point isn't exactly at the right place, then the geometric figures cannot be drawn. Everything is situated exactly at the right place. To get a clear picture overall I got an article from Bert that contained a few illustrations in which he fully describes how one thing is connected to the other.

Interesting too, that Assen was the site of the Netherlands first recorded crop circle, way back in 1590, by Robert Plott, an English Professor at Oxford University. It was reported that a grass circle had appeared on the night of August 18th of that year, although locals reported seeing men and women with cloven hooves dancing and it was put down to the activities of Petter Gross-petter.

Back to basic

What is it that makes crop circles such a fascinating phenomenon? No doubt the mysterious and inexplicable aspects play a major role here, but is that all? How can it be explained that people become so fascinated merely by looking at them? Even when they don't know a single thing about the crop formations, the symbols nevertheless seem to stir up interest. The question why this is, has kept me occupied for many years now. There's something about the pictograms that has some kind of hypnotising effect on people. But why?

From the very first crop circle formations, people like John Martineau and Wolfgang Schindler have worked with the geometry. They mostly aimed at the 'outside' of the pictograms. Until 1992 many formations indeed could be described by no more than five-fold geometry. But in 1992 the formations changed, and these simplistic geometrical explanations no longer held. Later Gerald Hawkins intensively studied the various elements within the crop circles. He found strong indications for the existence of diatonic ratios in the patterns. Although all these results are indeed fascinating, they weren't enough for me, to be honest. There had to be more. A more fundamental basis; and I found it. Many crop circles are built on simple but enlightening geometry. Geometry that provides us with certain results, certain derivatives, such as the findings of Martineau, Schindler and Hawkins. Geometry that is the basis, the source, the cause of their findings. The internal geometry of crop circles.

It all started with my attempts to reconstruct certain formations on paper by means of a ruler and a pair of compasses. I didn't use the ruler to measure, only to draw straight lines. I was therefore working with simplistic construction. The results were fascinating:

1. All formations I studied turned out to have exactly the same basic pattern.

2. All elements in a formation (and, as a result, all internal proportions as well) are not coincidental, but strictly results of their construction.

3. The necessary construction points (epicentres of used circles) can never be found in standing crop. This is how it works.

The above-mentioned basic pattern looks like this:

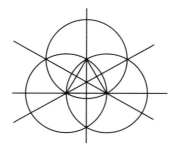

From this basic pattern many formations can be constructed. In this book I will explain how this basic pattern can be made. Let's now try to reconstruct a formation, a relatively simple one. Let's try the

Harlequin formation of 1997. Via several simple construction steps we come to this diagram:

This diagram shows an equilateral triangle, constructed in the three circles necessary to make the basic pattern and is the same as we can see in the Harlequin formation. Please notice the circle constructed neatly in the triangle. It's the same circle as those three constructed on the corners. Coincidence? The inner circle in the formation fits exactly in the equilateral triangle of the basic pattern. Coincidence? The end result looks like this:

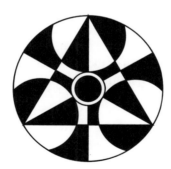

I must admit that this is a relatively simple and obvious formation. The next formation however shows us something a little different. Starting off with the same basic pattern we can reconstruct the following through a mere 15 simple steps:

It seems a variety of lines and circles, but in reality it is the internal geometry of the following pictogram:

In spite of the complex character of this formation, it can be constructed without trampling the standing crop. The following diagram shows the position of the necessary construction points. As you can see they all lie within the flattened crop.

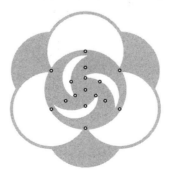

Some construction points lie exactly on the edge of the standing crop. It all fits just perfectly. If, for instance, the central circle had been just a little bit smaller, the formation could not have been made without damaging the standing crop. 'Luckily', the central circle has the perfect shape. Coincidence? We see the same principle when looking at the following formation. Starting off from the basic pattern we reconstruct through this:

this beauty:

And here as well we find the necessary construction points exactly on the edge of the standing crop.

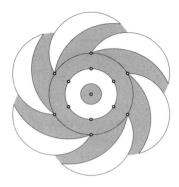

If the inner circle of the standing crop had been just a tiny bit bigger, this formation could not have been constructed without damaging the standing crop. But also this formation has the perfect size. Coincidence?

The formation of Etchilhampton of 1997 leads us even further. Via many steps we are able to reconstruct the final pattern, which shows the following construction points:

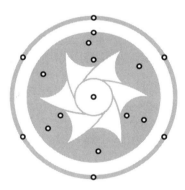

In order to construct this formation, we need several points that lie relatively far from the centre. This could have been a problem, but the ring around the formation brought help. Coincidence? Inside the formation the outer construction point also lies just in the flattened crop. Coincidence?

Crop Circles, Gods and their Secrets

Does this mean that we should only be focusing on the construction points? No. These points are merely one of many indicators that show us that the crop circle formations are formed via an extremely precise geometric pattern. They are made with geometric principles that are very well known to us.

What can we do with this knowledge? What does it tell us? One of the things is that, since they are all created from the same basic pattern, we can compare them with each other. For instance, we can compare their size, thanks to the basic pattern, which enabled us to superimpose the various formations. Moreover, now that we know their internal geometry, we can make them three-dimensional. And as we saw before in the basic pattern, every crop circle formation is based on an equilateral triangle, which is a tetrahedron three-dimensionally. By means of the above-mentioned geometry, the pictograms can be turned into three-dimensional figures based on mere tetrahedrons!

Every single element inside a formation is related by definition to all other elements inside that formation because of this geometry. Diatonic ratios are a logic result of this. But it goes even further. Every single element of a formation can be related to every single element of another formation!

So far, we have only looked at six-fold geometry. But what about five-fold geometry that we find, for instance, in the Star of Bethlehem from 1997? By means of the basic pattern this is how we can arrive at fivefold geometry;

Via a couple of construction phases we can construct this figure;

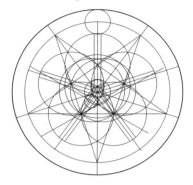

which leads us directly to;

Here too we notice that all construction points fit neatly inside the formation.

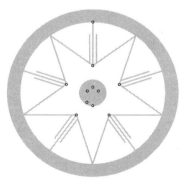

Crop Circles, Gods and their Secrets

If the inner circle were one inch smaller, we would have had a problem. Coincidence?

What you just saw is only the surface of the fascinating world of the crop circles' inner geometry. What I found out goes a lot further than described on these pages. For instance, it can be proved that Avebury's Web is an amalgamation between five- and six-fold geometry. Both geometries are interlocking in this extraordinary formation. Perhaps this perfect geometry is not telling us anything. Perhaps it is just needed to make the pictograms beautifully harmonic, which has a hypnotising effect on people. Perhaps the fact that the construction points are never in the standing crop is done on purpose to show us we're on the right track with this form of geometric analysis. Perhaps it is meant to focus our attention on the inner space rather than the surrounding matrix.

Music in crop circles?

As we have been able to see in Bert Janssen's story in which he sets apart the geometry of a few of the crop circle formations, certain geometric patterns are used by the crop circle makers in the crop formations. Gerald Hawkins, an American professor is another person who has researched the geometry of crop circle formations. Professor Hawkins is affiliated with the University of Boston in Washington D.C. It was in the '60sthat Hawkins subjected the geometry of Stonehenge to a thorough analysis. Over the years Hawkins has occupied himself with the crop circle phenomenon, and he noticed that there were diatonic relationships hidden within some of the crop circles. It all began with the three circles originating in 1988 close to Corhampton (Hampshire, England). Hawkins discovered that the relative position of the three circles was such that with the assistance of only three lines he could join all three circles (see illustration next page).

With other so-called triplets these identifying marks have been ascertained. In the meantime this identifying mark has become known

as 'Hawkins first theory'. Hawkins continued on and also formulated three other theories that have to do with plural geometry.

'Hawkins second theory' is the triplicate geometry. This triplicate geometry does not mean that the geometry consists of three identical symmetrical portions. The following drawing clarifies what is understood by the word triplicate geometry.

As a result of the calculations it seems that the inside circle is 4 times smaller than the outside circle. A surface area ratio of 4:1.

Hawkins following theory is the quadruple geometry. It is a square enclosed by a circle while there is another circle within the square. The ratio of the two circles is 2:1. The outside circle is therefore two times larger than the inside one.

Crop Circles, Gods and their Secrets

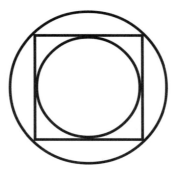

Hawkins fourth theory isn't a pentagon but an even sided hexagon. Here the ratios of the two circles equates to 4:3 (see image next page)

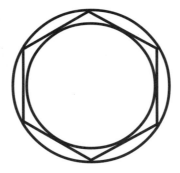

Hawkins four theories cannot be traced back to Euclidean geometry. There isn't even anything mentioned in modern day mathematical literature that refers to this.

Hawkins noticed that the surface area ratios correspond to the white keys of a piano's keyboard. Many of the geometrical ratios seemed to be identical to those frequencies of a musical scale. For example the pitch of a piano's chord is determined by the amount of times the chord vibrates (i.e. the frequency).

The following drawings show the different diatonic relationships that Hawkins found and how he projected them onto the keyboard of a piano.

Diatonic Ratio's							
First Octave	1 C	9/8 D	5/4 E	4/3 F	3/ G	5/3 A	15/8 B
Fourth Octave	2 H	9/4 I	5/2 J	8/3 K	3 L	10/3 M	15/4 N
Second Oc	3 O	9/2 P	5 Q	16/3 R	6 S	20/3 T	15/2 U
Third Octave	4 V	9 W	10 X	32/3 Y	12 Z	40/3 A	15 B
Piano notes	C	D	E	F	G	A	B

Hawkins researched the following crop circles for diatonic relationships and discovered from them that there were initials to be found in each one of them. Who did these initials belong to? Research pointed out that these initials could only be applied to the list of the first 25 presidents of the 'Society for Physical Research of London'. The T number that is stated behind the mentioned formations belongs to Colin Andrew's catalogues. The list is as follows:

1988 Corhampton	T4	CR Charles Richet
1989 Winterborn Stoke	T1-FL5	BC Boyd Carpenter
1990 Longwood Estate	T26	HS Henry Sidgwick
1990 Fordham Place	T283	JS Lord Rayleigh (John Strutt)
1992 Oliver's Castle	T86	WC William Crookes
1992 Sompting	T167	HS Henry Sidgwick
1993 Etchilhampton	T221	CF Camille Flammarion
1993 Hog's Back Hill	T242	OL Oliver Lodge

1993 Uffington W Horse   T313   OL Oliver Lodge
1996 Littlebury Green   T448   FM Frederic Myers

The chance that the initials that Hawkins found could be matched to the list of the presidents of the Society for Physical Research of London is a 1chance in 1.7 billion .

The mystery of the dead flies

In all the years that people have been occupied with the crop circle phenomenon many extraordinary incidents have been observed along with the discovery of the white substances. One of the most remarkable findings is one by Dr. Janet Ossebaard. She is a member of the Dutch C.C.C.S. and has been involved with world-wide research on crop circle formations for many years.

On the 17th of July 1998 she discovered something very strange in a circle close to Cher Hill, Wiltshire, England. This concerned some black flies that were glued with their proboscis to the crop stems as if they had daubed themselves with a good dose of 'crazy glue' before brushing down upon the stalks with their mouth-parts of glue. Besides the flies that looked like they had exploded there were flies that seemed as if they were in a state of shock. Their legs and wings were stretched out and the flies were connected to the grain with only their proboscis in contact with the plant.

For some considerable time there has been the suspicion that there is some unknown energy responsible for the formation of crop circles. It seemed as if this energy was also responsible for the flies' state of shock (see photograph next page).

Later on Janet heard from another crop circle researcher that he had already come across dead flies in a formation in 1994 only he had never mentioned it. In the near future more and more strange inexpicable events will present themselves in the appearance of world-wide crop circle formations. These events will need an explanation,

and a solution. They will need to be researched, investigated and precisely worked out. Many of even the most bizarre will probably eventually present a mundane explanation.

Currently most of the research is directed to charting as many of the different formations as possible along with their individual peculiarities down to the smallest details. Details such as dead flies, white powder and the latent geometry in crop circles. The question is, is this the only thing that is concealed in these spectacular formations or are there still pieces of a hidden message harboured in the many formations? To me the question if there is 'coded' information or messages hidden within the crop circles is superfluous, because I *know* that there are for sure.

2 Crop circles analysed in numbers and letters

Crop circles, the Seven Seals

A few days after my discovery of the pictogram in Brummen, which started as a journey from the airport in Teuge, the picture of my discovery was published in the local newspaper. A few days after the appearance of this phenomenon in our local newspaper a man who told me he had a lot more information regarding the crop circle phenomenon contacted me. Full of curiosity I went to see him and we spoke for a long time. Amongst many other things, he told me that the three connecting circles were either a sign or a seal of an Angel. There are eight of these signs or seal. Who are these eight.... and particularly what are they? After I received a few key words from him and some tips regarding where I should continue to search from more information I left. Unfortunately he could not share all his knowledge with me due to some 'secret teachings'. Such organisations have held their secrets for years and don't just give them away to anyone. On my way out he wished me a pleasant day and even said "You will figure it out, you are on the right path". Totally taken aback by his comment I bid him good day.

After a long time of thoughtful consideration I started on my quest of discovery. But really where do you start? The local library seemed as good a place as any. After consulting many books, calling many numbers, conducting many more conversations and what seemed to me to be the most important of all, logical thinking, I came to the following conclusion: Signs are seals and vice versa. At a certain moment I arrived at King Solomon. The most well known seal of King Solomon is the 'Star of David'. According to the Jewish Historical Museum in Amsterdam it is a 'Hexagon amulet invoking God in the name of the seal of Solomon'. Apparently King Solomon had a large number of these seals including the seals of the Angels. According to my informant the eight seals of the Angels are the same seals that Solomon had available for his own use. The Sefer Yetzirah (The Book of Creation, translated from Hebrew into English by Aryeh Kaplan) is the oldest and most secretive writing of the Cabalistic texts, which talk about the 'Seals of the Planets', and about the 'Seals of the Planetary Angels' and the 'Seals of the Seven Planets'. All these represent seven seals which in their turn all correspond with each other. There is a Cabalistic amulet whose origin is unknown on which the same signs have been produced as on the Seals of the Angels in the Sefer Yetzirah. Do you suppose the Seven Angel Seals plus the main seal, the Star of David of Solomon, only belonged to Solomon or in other words are they not one and the same? In all of history have different peoples given a different name to one and the same thing?

The case is the same as far as the gods are concerned, specifically speaking of Thoth. The Egyptians called him Thoth the messenger of the gods and the keeper of knowledge. The Romans knew him as Mercury while in South-America he lived under the name of Quetzalcoatl. In Mexico his name was Viracocha. In Greece he was known as Hermes, Hermes is the hero of the Rosicrucians and that brings us back to the Rosicrucians with all their of old collected knowledge. (Later I will introduce the other names that the god Thoth has).

Of course there are more Angels than these seven, but these are the seven of whom there are portrayals. A portrayal is something physical (a portrait), something you can see, even in a field of grain. So if through the years various pictograms have appeared, such asthe formation of Landgraaf in 1996 and various similar pictograms in England then I cannot deny myself the impression made upon me by the various signs/seals of the Angels that have been created as pictograms in the fields repeatedly found to be constructed in a similar manner by two or more circles, lines or half Moons connected by a straight line (see illustrations next page).

Crop Circles, Gods and their Secrets

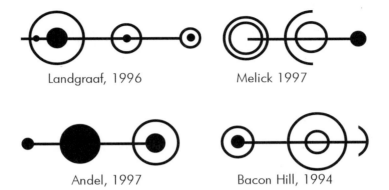

Landgraaf, 1996   Melick 1997

Andel, 1997   Bacon Hill, 1994

If indeed there are crop circles that show the Seal of an Angel there should be someway to trace the name of the Angel concerned. There could also be combined seals. This means that one seal/pictogram could be created from several different seals. Research for these types of seals/pictograms is in full swing.

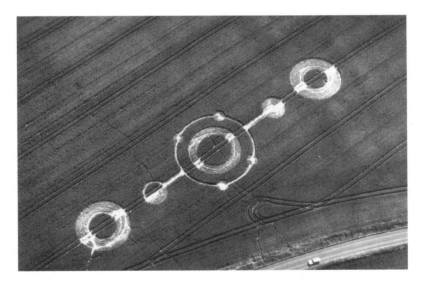

As far as I am concerned Hebrew is the language of the gods who handed the stone tablets over to Moses. In the Hebrew language the origin of a word can be traced back to one letter. Therefore an

Angel could represent one letter, which could therefore coincide with a note or a tone. A note or a tone is sound and sound is vibration. Everything revolves around vibration. Everything IS vibration. In this respect if one knows the exact vibration of everything then one could change a wooden table into an iron table and vice versa. If in turn a crop circle formation gives off certain vibrations to heal our Earth then it should be possible to locate the leylines and to see where there are negative 'flows' of energy running through the Earth and be able to eliminate them with 'better' vibrations.

Seals in ancient times

In ancient times many different signs, seals or amulets were used for healing, exorcism or to conjure up ghosts and/or demons. It would be very interesting, if you got permission from a farmer to reproduce a pictogram in his field that was proven to be full of warmth, love and positive energy, to see if there would be that kind of energy evident in the replica. If you reproduced the 'wrong' kind of seal you could conjure up the 'wrong things'. As I mentioned earlier this could be the explanation as to why there were not very many crop circles in 1998. It is a possibility that the hoax that was discovered in Zierikzee on the 17th of July 1997 was a negative energy formation. When I look at the picture it gives me the feeling that the formation 'takes', draws something into it. If you lay the picture of the three-armed Julia Set spiral beside it, the spiral gives me the feeling that it is a 'giving' formation.

One and all sevens

To elaborate further on the Seven Seals I just wish to briefly bring up the Seven Seals of Atlantis. Once again seven seals. The Bible also talks about Seven Seals in Revelations 5: 1-5 where the scroll is closed with the Seven Seals. Seven is a holy number, which recurs very often. The Sefer Yetzirah talks about the Seven Universes, Firmaments, Earths, Seas, Rivers, Deserts and Days. The Seven

Weeks are also briefly discussed 'between Pesach and Shavuot', being the Seven Weeks, Sabbaticals and Jubilees, each described separately. Earlier on I have already mentioned the Seven Angels with their matching Seven Planets. This book also talks about the seven holes in the human head.

Besides the one great Sphinx in Egypt there are six more just as magnificent as the main sphinx so if you add that up we come to seven again. In all religions seven is the holy number. The ancient Sumerians knew of the symbol that had been given to the Earth by the Anunnaki/Nephilim. It was a symbol of... seven dots, because in the celestial bodies orbiting outside of our solar system Pluto is the first planet that one runs into. The Earth is number 7. Seven is a holy number. As far as I am concerned the Seven Seals recur just a bit too regularly. Likewise the pictogram of 1997 in Brummen adds up to seven circles and the word 'coincidence' does not exist in my vocabulary.

The Seven Seals of Atlantis

According to a good friend of mine, Hylke Welling, who has been occupied, with the study of Atlantis and Egypt for more than 30 years, the Seven Seals are the period in which Atlantis lies submerged in the sea. Edgar Cayce predicted that Atlantis would re-surface at some point. The question is when and will it literally rise above the water or will only the knowledge and reminder of who we are and from whom we have evolved resurface? Maybe the most important of all is that it will teach us what we still need to learn in this great time of change. According to Mr. Welling the Seven Seals could be associated with the constellations of the Zodiacs that we have had since the downfall of Atlantis. If you start counting back then you have Pisces, Aries, Taurus, Gemini, Cancer and Leo. As mentioned before the ancient Sumerians counted 2160 years for one constellation of the Zodiac, while the Egyptians counted 2150 years. Today experts have figured out that this cycle is 2148 years long. If you multiply that amount by six constellations then you arrive at approx. 13,000 years ago. Around that time was when Atlantis perished. This is also the time when the age of Leo came upon us ca. 10,970 BC until 8810 BC.

We are now in the period of the seventh zodiac sign (constellation = seal). We are in Aquarius, the 11th sign of the zodiac symbolised by the Water Bearer who represents change. Does that mean that during this Age of Aquarius that Atlantis will resurface? I don't know, but with all the recent discoveries in Egypt and all the other business that seems to be surfacing it could very well be possible that this would indeed be the case. According to various people involved with these particular studies it has been stated that underneath the Great Pyramid of Giza a twelve-story building has been found. A sarcophagus was found there with the body of a man, wrapped in a long pink and white robe, within it. A cartouche on his chest states the name of Osiris. He has entered a state of changed consciousness by which he appears to be dead, but he is definitely not dead.

In his book 'What did the Mayans know' the Dutch author, Peter Toonen describes that Drunvalo Melchizedek received 'messages' from Thoth himself. Drunvalo comes from another dimension and is a so-called 'walk –in'. This means that someone else reserved a body for him until Drunvalo was prepared to 'take over' the body. Melchizedek swam around on a water-enriched planet close to Sirius (also known as the Dog Star) instructed by dolphins as to what was going on on Earth, before he came here.

After the fall of Atlantis Thoth travelled with a sort of spaceship to Egypt, Peru and Tibet. He went there as a sort of Moses to place his Ten Commandments 'The Emerald Tablets'. These 'Emerald Tablets' contain all the knowledge and wisdom of Thoth before the fall of Atlantis. Atlantis had a much higher degree of civilisation then we have at this moment. If all the knowledge of Thoth that was embedded on the twelve tablets is ever found then you could assume that Atlantis would 'resurface'. The actual physical Atlantis will not resurface but only the knowledge.

Crop Circles, Gods and their Secrets

Thoth placed these tablets in the Great Halls of Amenti (literally it means 'dead' but actually it is an altered state of being known as sleeping) under the ground in the neighbourhood of the Sphinx. Immediately after that he, Thoth, built the pyramids (ca. 14,000 BC) and then he departed to the highest pitch (vibration) of the Fourth Dimension.

According to old Arabic myths the pyramids were built to preserve all knowledge that had been learned thus far. The story goes that the gods instructed the people in many areas such as in; agriculture, astrology, astrology, geometry, etc. A flood was predicted to occur and the people asked the gods if the knowledge they had received from them could be preserved. Therefore the construction of the pyramids in which lays the great knowledge of the gods. Is that the knowledge that Thoth placed there to be preserved? What exactly is this knowledge and what could we learn from it if it were ultimately exposed to the public?

Are the crop circle formations and pictograms with all their variants and figures a language, which we do not yet understand? Are the crop circles messages from another dimension? Are there truly Angels at work here leaving their 'Seals' or prints behind in the shapes of crop circle formations? Will everything return and fall into place after the many needed changes are made or will we mess up again, like we have in the past? Will history repeat itself?

Talk to us

After this journey of discovery several things have become quite clear to me. I really do believe there are 'Angels' (in the Sanskrit language angels or half-gods are referred to as 'Devas') working amongst us to show us through crop circles that there is more between heaven and Earth than we have ever thought there was up until now. Sometimes, but just very seldom 'they' tell us exactly what is the matter or rather what was the matter. Together with a piece of the history of man 'they' tell us their name and the role 'they' played in making that part of history. I am convinced that if you know a lot about the past then you are better prepared for the future and are able to cope with what you are in for.

One of the most remarkable things that I found, is the event that took place close to Milk Hill, nearby Alton Barnes and Alton Priors, Wiltshire. In August of 1991, the American Eric Beckjord wrote with the permission of the landowner the text 'TALK TO US' in the grain. By the middle of August of the same year there was a reply in what seemed to us as an odd and strange unknown language in the grain field. They were odd 'letters' or symbols that had been flattened into the grain, the formation had a total length of 55 metres and were 5.5 metres high. Michael Green, an English archaeologist who is the founder and president of the CCCS (Centre for Crop Circle Studies) identified these 'letters' as a form of ancient Hebrew.

From right to left it says; Phehthi or Ptah (the Egyptian god of creation) and Ea-cheche or Ea-Enki (the Sumerian god of wisdom; friend of the people). This is a very interesting fact because in the next chapter I believe that a very substantial link can be made between two very different formations. A link that I believe has never been

Crop Circles, Gods and their Secrets

made before, which is all the more reason to comprehend the past first before you can even begin to attempt to decipher the mysteries of the past and the future. To whom do these names belong that were found in the inscription? Who are 'Ea, Enki and Ptah' actually? Are we conceivably speaking of beings from another planet or gods or 'simply' mythological names from ancient times? To be able to explain this we need to have some other information before we can understand the rest and be able to place the link between the two formations.

What can Sitchin tell us?

A few years ago I came in contact with a gentleman by the name of Evert Poorterman. Full of fire he told me that that he had already got his hands on Zecharia Sitchin's book a few years ago. It was the book 'The Twelfth Planet' that, and I quote: 'Uranus was discovered in 1781. After having observed an unknown planet for 50 years, one figured out, with help of mathematical calculations, how to locate this planet. Neptune was discovered in 1846. At the end of the 19th century it became clear that there had to be another planet that was disturbing the orbits of both Neptune and Uranus. The mystery was solved when Pluto was discovered in 1930. In 1986 images of Pluto were directed to us through the *Voyager* space probe and it appeared that the planet was much smaller than we had presumed. But 'something' large was still disturbing Neptune and Uranus' orbit, but what was it? (In 1978 astronomers from the Marine Observatory in Washington were already claiming that Pluto was much smaller than what had generally been calculated until now. Pluto can therefore no longer be seen as the only cause of irregularities surrounding the orbit of Neptune. In June of 1979 Zecharia Sitchin was told that the search for a larger planet was underway. Astronomers have now been looking for more than twenty years).'

This as yet not located planet is three times larger in mass than our planet Earth. Astronomers have calculated that its orbital speed in revolving around the Sun is 3600 years. Presumably this planet passed us around 200 BC on a very eccentric orbit.

What does NASA know?

In 1982 NASA went on record to state that there was a possibility that a planet X existed. Furthermore they stated that there was a mysterious object so far away that it bordered on the outside of our furthest planets.

In 1983 a group of astronomers together with NASA launched a satellite by the name of IRAS. IRAS stands for 'Infrared Astronomical Satellite'. After having discovered several unknown comets one also encountered a large, unknown heavenly body. Apparently it was just as big as Jupiter and it was part of our solar system. The Washington Post had published a summary from the interview with the man who was in charge of the IRAS project. He stated that they had indeed discovered a large unknown heavenly body with the IRAS, possibly as large as Jupiter. It was a possibility that it would come so close to the Earth that it would become part of our solar system. The great unknown was apparently found in the direction of the constellation Orion. According to the manager of the IRAS that is all they knew. In the late eighties these facts were submerged into the well known and possibly even developed by NASA 'extinguisher of information' to quieten the whole matter but now that the new millennium has arrived there are several scientists who have not forgotten that a planet X exists and their curiosities returned. In his book 'The Alien Logbook' Jim Marrs gives an excellent translation of what the letters NASA stands for: 'Never A Straight Answer'. As we have stated earlier, there was something that caused irregularities in Neptune's orbit. What caused these disturbances? Could it be the planet which Sitchin talks about as a result of his findings from the translations of the ancient tablets found in Nineveh?

Planet X; Nibiru, the planet of the gods

In the beginning of time when our solar system came into being and when it was still young and out of balance a strange planet passed our still in the making solar system. The intruder was sucked into our solar system by the great gravitational pull of our farthest planets. This intruder, who was later named Nibiru, came closer and closer to Tiamat due to the gravitational pull of the Sun. One of the 4 Moons that belonged to the intruder struck Tiamat and split the planet. Due to this occurrence Tiamat's orbit was still between Mars and Jupiter but during the next passage of Nibiru the planet of the gods crashed into the already damaged Tiamat. Tiamat then split into two and 'exploded' to its new orbit between Mars and Venus. The one half of Tiamat became the asteroid belt and the other half became the Earth. Since that time Nibiru is part of our solar system and waits there for us every 3600 years.

The inhabitants of Nibiru are the Anunnaki. In Sumerian AN.UNNA.KI means 'Those who came from the heavens to the Earth'. In Hebrew the Anunnaki were called the Nephilim which means 'Those who descended' almost the exact same definition as in Sumerian. In ancient times Sumeria was written as KI.EN.GIR. by the early Sumerians which literally means 'the land of the man with rockets'.

In the eyes of the ancient Sumerians the inhabitants of Nibiru were considered to be 'gods' with all their vehicles, weapons and knowledge. The leader of the Anunnaki peoples who first came to Earth was Ea. Ea means, 'god of water'. According to Zecharia Sitchin, Ea landed more than 450,000 years ago in the Persian Gulf at the latitude of the present Kuwait. The flight control centre of the Anunnaki was found in Mesopotamia, which, in the Bible and in mythology became known as E.DIN that is Eden.

I consciously say, 'according to the calculations of Sitchin' because there are more calculations that have given more precise estimates. We must not forget that Sitchin performed these assessments at the end of the 60s. Naturally he overlooked a few things. Nowadays these are things that could suddenly have a total different meaning. Alan Alford figured out in his book 'Gods of a new millennium' that the gods came to Earth around 270,000 BC. Alford wanted his new chronology to be in agreement with the biblical timetable of Adam to

Noah and in agreement with the Babylonian and Sumerian lists of Kings. His computations also had to be in agreement with the chronology of the Egyptian gods before the great flood as Manetho drew it out at that time. Alford based his calculations on a 'SAR' (period) of 2160 years while Sitchin did it with a 'SAR' period of 3600 years. Based on Alford calculations I am doubtful that the revolution period of the Twelfth Planet, Nibiru will actually be 3600 years considering that in the Sumerian counting system you write 2160 as 3600.

On which calculation is the Nibiru's orbit based? The term 'SAR' is sometimes applicable to Nibiru. 'SAR' also meant 'supreme ruler' by which the people of Nibiru were referring to the 'boss', otherwise known as Anu. The term 'SAR' was also used to represent the number 3600 and was named in several contexts as the 'complete cycle' In reference to these indications Sitchin has concluded that Nibiru has an orbit around the Sun of 3600 years. Further on in the section on 'A return of the gods in 2012?' I made a calculation in which it is apparent that Nibiru will make its return into our solar system in 2012. Alford's conclusions explain the sudden change over from Homo Erectus to Homo Sapiens around 200,000 years ago. This change over was so sudden that it has left modern day science baffled as they are still trying to come up with theories to convince us that it was a natural process of evolution. To me it seems as if Alford's calculations are more logical than those of Sitchin because it doesn't seem possible to me that one 'god' could come to a planet explore it and then after a 'short period' of 250,000 years create a 'slave'. What seems to be more logical is that the gods already created a worker after a 'mere' 70,000 years and did not continue to do the work themselves. The Homo Sapiens date back about 200,000 years. Thoth 'told' Drunvalo Melchizedek himself that the exact date was 200,207 years ago.

According to the translations of the old clay tablets the Anunnaki were looking for gold. Certainly not because they thought it was beautiful but for pure necessity. They had abused nature and technology on Nibiru, which resulted in the thinning of the atmosphere.

The atmosphere was not only for breathing but it also served as a buffer zone to keep in the heat that the planet radiated out from within. After many years of having extracted the gold themselves from the planet the llabouring folk' complained to the gods. The labour was too heavy for them. A solution had to be found. Discussions took place between the gods and the final decision made was that genetic manipulation would take place between an Anunnaki and a then inhabitant of the Earth known as Homo Sapiens to create the LU.LU. In ancient Sumerian texts the word LU.LU literally means; 'the mixed one'. Adam was born in the laboratory of the gods, inhabitants of another planet.

It may sound a bit odd if we talk about genetic manipulation in ancient times but I would like to point out to you that scientists are involved with the very same accomplishment today as those gods of thousands of years ago. Genetic manipulation and cloning is something we are capable of today so why is it so hard to grasp the fact that a superior civilisation has mastered this feat thousands of years ago? We cannot comprehend that there is a civilisation out there that mastered 'our' techniques many, many years ago. But just think if our scientists are capable of this already what will they be up to in roughly ten or twenty years? Perhaps they will also be able to create a LU.LU?

The coming of the 'great flood'

What happened for the rest is history. The gods were disappointed in humans because of the fact that mankind had discovered how to mate and duplicate therefore being rather preoccupied with this act instead of thinking of how to please the gods. Humans multiplied and before you knew it there were too many people. The gods decided to let the people succumb, considering they were aware of the fact that the planet Nibiru would be coming closer to the Earth in its orbit than previous passages and that because of this it would create a great flood. I am taking into consideration that it is possible that the gravitational pull of Nibiru caused the unstable Antarctic ice cap to come out of balance, causing it to crash into the sea therefore creating the great flood. This hypothesis could also confirm Charles Hapgood's theory of the shifting of the Earth's crust. His theory presumes that the Earth's crust can shift over a liquid inner core. It could also explain why there was such an abrupt ending to the ice age and all the consequences of it. In 1953 Albert Einstein already wrote that it was possible that due to the centrifugal forces of the turning Earth an iceberg could start to shift. This gigantic, heavy, shifting ice mass can project its strength onto the Earth's crust which in turn can cause the liquid inner core to start shifting. If by 'coincidence' there also happens to be a planet passing by with an enormous gravitational pull, in combination with all these above-mentioned forces, along with unknown to us factors, a calamity is bound to occur.

The gods knew of the coming flood but they had agreed not to inform the unsuspecting mankind. Enki could not stand by and let this happen so he informed his trusty servant Noah as to what was about to happen (in ancient versions of the great flood Noah was known as Utnapishtim). Utnapishtim was the Babylonian Noah. Enki couldn't speak directly to his servant because he knew he would be accused of betrayal by the other gods instead he chose to pretend he was talking to a screen of reeds. His trusty servant was standing on the other side and knew exactly what would happen and built a boat according to Enki's explicit instructions.

However Sitchin informs us that the word 'boat' has not been translated correctly. The Biblical stories regularly speak of an ark, while the Biblical term, teba, stems from the base word 'Sunken'. From this Sitchin concluded that Enki instructed Noah to build a 'submarine with a roof above it and a roof underneath it' and to hermetically seal it off with tough, hardy pitch. The 'boat' was to be let into the water when there was thunder in the skies. The thunder was actually the rockets that belonged to the Anunnaki soaring through the skies in their ever so quick disappearance from the Earth because they did not want to be swallowed up by the same great flood that was to wipe out mankind.

Thanks to Enki, Noah and his family were able to survive the great flood. After the ark grounded on Mount Ararat Noah offered a sacrifice of roast meat. The gods smelled the scent of the 'prehistoric barbecue' and descended to Earth. Enlil was furious with Enki because there were survivors. Once he smelled the aroma of the meat and ate some of the offering he also had to admit that the gods could no longer live without the people and the animals.

The cross, the symbol of the Nibiru

The ancient Sumerians already knew of this twelfth planet, Nibiru and its inhabitants the Anunnaki that belongs to our solar system. The Sumerians called this planet 'the planet of the crossing' thus the symbol of the cross representing it (see illustration).

Throughout centuries there have been many crosses in various religions and orders that were derived from the cross/symbol of the Nibiru. Below you will find several examples of a normal cross (the plus sign) and a derivative of that. You can find a lot of these kinds of crosses throughout history, amongst those are the Rosicrucians and the KnightsTemplar (see illustrations next page).

Even the Swastika, one of the oldest and most mysterious symbols of mankind could be a derivative from the Nibiru. For thousands of years the swastika has been used as a symbol of the revolving Sun. The Javanese give it the name 'Balok Bosok' from 'Mbalik Bosok', which means 'locking out the evil'. Further derivatives of the cross from the planet of the gods are the Celtic cross and the cross, as we know it today. In my opinion the present day religions have their cross thanks to the 'Twelfth Planet' and according the Sumerians this was 'the planet of thwarting' (see illustrations).

The gods and their names

After the flood Ea received the authority of leadership over Egypt, while his brother Enlil became leader of Mesopotamia. Ea was to dry up Egypt and make it liveable after the flood. His name changed to Enki while he was there. He did not change his name himself considering the fact that he had many titles and nicknames. This name was given to him. Enki means, 'Lord of the Land'. His Egyptian name was Ptah. He was also known as Aa in Egypt. Enki/Ptah had a son named Thoth who was the Egyptian god of scientific knowledge, mathematics and the calendar. He was the divine writer that kept up the books of the gods and the keeper of the secrets of the Pyramids. He was also the god of time, the chronicle writer of the Eons (very long time periods), the trustee of the Akasha Chronicles and the trustee of the Karma (later I will talk more about Thoth and all his names). He was the god of the Moon calendar while his brother Ra was the god of the Sun calendar. Ra was Enki/Ptah's oldest son. In Sumeria Thoth was known as Ningisjzidda while Ra was known as Marduk. Ningisjzidda means, 'Lord of the artefact of life', which meant he had the knowledge to resurrect the dead. The symbol that belonged to Thoth/Ningisjzidda was two intertwined snakes that he had inherited from his father Enki/Ptah. According to Sitchin the symbol of the two snakes twisted around each other is derived from the double helix structure of DNA (see illustration).

Genetic manipulation

At the time father Ptah/Enki was involved with genetic manipulations. Thoth/Ningisjzidda was fully aware of the genetic manipulations of his father while Ra/Marduk, with his lust for power, knew much less about these. Together with his half sister Ninharsag, who was a biologist and a medical doctor, Ptah/Enki was responsible for the creation of Adam. It was necessary that a 'human' be created because the god's workload was becoming too heavy. The 'human' could take over the heavy labour and therefore serve the gods. If we compare this story to the Bible and open it up to Genesis 1:26 the Bible becomes more clear than ever. In Genesis 1:26 it says 'Then God said, let US make man in OUR image, in OUR likeness' but to whom is being referred as 'God'? To whom is God actually speaking? And who is this US? In the original Hebrew version of the Bible instead of God it says, Elohim, which is the plural of Eloah, the Lord. So actually in the above-mentioned Bible quotation it says 'and the GODS said; let US make man in OUR image, in Our likeness'. The US refers to Ptah/Enki who together with his half sister Ninharsag are actually responsible for 'our' creation such as the actual translations from the Sumerians already tell us. Have there actually been genetic manipulations to intervene with the development of man?

Milk Hill once again

In reference to the above-mentioned 'creation' of Ptah/Enki of Adam it is obviously rather remarkable that a crop circle formation, which was found close to East Field nearby Alton Priors. Once again it was close to Alton-Barnes where five years previously the inscription I had mentioned earlier had appeared. This crop circle formation is called the Double Helix because it looks identical to the human DNA spiral (see illustration). The total length of this formation was 197.5 metres long and it had 89 circles in it!

The odd thing is that to the question 'TALK TO US' the answer was: Phehthi or Ptah and Ea-cheche or Ea-Enki, and haven't we just seen now that Enki and Ptah are one and the same 'person'. Ea when he landed in the Persian Gulf, Ptah when in Egypt, and Enki in Egypt. And isn't it odd that the same Ptah/Enki kept himself busy with genetic manipulations in the past? What is even more remarkable is that an extra circle was found in the crop circle formation. This extra circle was found hidden under an already existing circle. Could this extra circle be 'missing link' between the gods and mankind? Is that the extra piece of DNA that is responsible for the fact that we only use a very small portion of our brain? Did the gods alter our DNA in comparison to theirs in earlier times? Are the gods amongst us again and are they responsible for the various crop circle formations? Is this their way, by means of crop circle formations, to make something obvious to us? If they do want to make something evident to us what is it then?

Milk Hill again, but different

As we read earlier the English archaeologist Michael Green translated the inscription at Milk Hill in 1991 as Phethi or Ptah and Ea-cheche or Ea-Enki. That Ea, Enki and Ptah or one and the same person is a fact which I have been able to set apart but what kept me occupied was the fact that did Michael Green translated the inscription as individual; letters or in the context of a sentence? I also doubted the correct translation of cheche as Enki mainly because it just didn't seem right to me. This was purely instinctive and I could not state specifically what it was that it did not make sense to me. I just had a feeling that the inscription said a whole lot more than the translation given by Green.

I came to that conclusion after I had engrossed myself in Hebrew. Hebrew is a language in which you can read the letters, the words and the sentences individually. Individual letters can form words with different meanings, as long as they are used in a word or in a sentence. You only need to take two Hebrew letters and you already have one or more words with one or more different meanings. This is in contrast to Western language where you need a grouping of letters to form a word. Michael Drosnin tells us in his book 'The Bible Code 'how you can decipher the Hebrew Bible with a computer program in order to be able to perform predictions. Amongst many other things you can read about the murder of Yitzhak Rabin in the Bible Code. Drosnin was able to recall the date and name of Kennedy's murderer through his decoding from the Bible Code.

Considering that I was not quite comfortable with Michael Green's translations I went with a picture and the appropriate inscription to

Ora van Oostende. Ora has mastered Hebrew scripture and the language. I showed her the picture, and after she examined the photograph she said that Michael Green's translation was correct but that he had only translated the old Hebrew letters. According to her there was no context to the inscription. Having read the inscription from right to left or vice versa it did not give her any insight as to something readable. Had Michael Green really translated everything there was to know? Were only the free standing letters translatable and nothing else? Were my intuitions deserting me? I suppose it could be true but something inside of me told me to approach this in a different manner. But how? After some contemplative and deep thought I discovered the answer.

Anamorphosis, also known as mirror, mirror on the wall...

Looking back it is truly amazing how ingeniously this inscription is 'written' in the grain. The ancient Hebrew letters are there in plain sight for everyone to read, but the hidden 'message' is not accessible to everyone. To be able to decipher that we needed to use a technique from Medieval Times (middle ages) which was known as 'Anamorphosis'. This technique was used to examine drawings in a way that you would not regularly use. For political reasons the drawings were made this way so that your enemy could not decipher the document, but that with the help of a mirror or foil, pasted on a hollow cylinder, you could look at the drawing. One only had to place the cylinder in the middle of the drawing and you could see and understand what was drawn. When we tried to decipher the inscription we did exactly the same thing they would have done in Medieval Times when an outsider was not allowed to know the contents of the message. The outsider was not aware of the 'mirror trick' and could not see the illustration. The inscription is written in exactly the same manner. An outsider cannot see which 'message' is noted there. Only the Hebrew letters, which have been translated by Green, were graphic but not the rest, not until we did the following. Instead of the plain, familiar inscription as noted below',

we placed a mirror on the left-hand side of the inscription we saw the following results appear; the same result is possible if you use the photo image of the inscription and hold it against the light.

The inscription, which was now magically transformed in front of our eyes, turned into a perfectly intelligible sentence. The result was even more remarkable than the final interpretations made by Green. In Hebrew it says 'Sewet chm anasim gadasim', which literally translated says; 'New Breed People'. In proper English you would say 'A New Breed of People'. A spectacular finding, especially because the name Enki can be read in the original inscription. Wasn't Enki the person who, amongst other things, was responsible for the creation of Adam?

In summary: to the question 'TALK TO US' various names representing the titles of Enki appears. In mirror image it says 'A NEW BREED OF PEOPLE', and five years later close to Milk Hill the DNA symbol (the double helix) appears. In other words you could say; 'WHO ARE YOU?' As a response you would get: 'I am Ea, also known as Enki or Ptah, and I was the one who was responsible for the creation of man through means of genetic manipulation!' Could we possibly use the sentence in different context? Let us go on and find out.

New clan from Adam...?

The question is which 'NEW BREED of PEOPLE' is meant here? Aren't we talking about what the gods did thousands of years ago? The gods placed the first human on the Earth with their genetic manipulations. So in other words you could say that with the creation of Adam 'A NEW BREED' came to Earth.

from Noah ...?

In mirror image the word cheche came out as 'chm'. In this sentence structure we could place an 'A' between the letters 'chm'. We then get the word 'Cham', which means; 'warmth'. In that context it therefore says; 'a NEW BREED of PEOPLE from CHAM!' But... who or what is Cham ? In the Bible Cham is Ham who is, together with his brothers Shem and Japheth, the sons of Noah. Together with his family, Noah was the only one who survived the great flood. In Genesis 9:18-19 one reads that: 'The sons of Noah who came out of the ark were Shem, Ham, and Japheth. (Ham was the father of Canaan.) These were the three sons of Noah, and from them came the people who scattered over the Earth.'... Are we (or the Jewish people) therefore the 'NEW BREED OF PEOPLE' because according to the Bible we stem from Ham, Shem and Japheth?

or...?

should we see the 'NEW BREED OF PEOPLE' as a 'new breed of the future'? In other words; nowadays more and more people are occupied with developing their spiritual self. More and more people have discovered that there is more between heaven and Earth than they had assumed up until this point. Does the upcoming transition into the fourth dimension have anything to do with this? Are we more conscious of everything? Are we going home?

Coffee and vowels

Still reflecting on the previously mentioned topic, on a beautiful April Sunday, I hopped on my motorbike to take a peaceful tour in the vicinity of my home. Wonderfully relaxed on my motorbike to my surprise (obviously too relaxed) I discovered I was already in the neighbourhood of Amersfoort ± 65 km away from my home. Since I was in the neighbourhood anyway I thought I would grab a cup of coffee at my friend's 'the walking encyclopaedia' home. He is otherwise known as Hylke Welling.

During the pleasure of a great cup of coffee the topic quickly landed on Egypt and the Egyptian Hieroglyphics. After awhile I told him I had received his copy of the stone circle with a diameter of 18 metres that could be seen in the Tenere desert in Nigeria. At approximately 1600 meters from the circle in every wind direction there was an arrow pointing away from it. The objective, the origin and the builders of it are unknown to us. I asked Hylke if he knew more about this but instead he told me something else. As usual on a regular basis Hylke is not in compliance with the current translations that originate from Egypt. His notion is that the scholars make quite a mess of things. He further went on to tell me that the Tenere desert should not be called as such but the Tanara desert. Similar to the Hebrew language the Egyptian language only has consonants and no vowels. The vowels you have to fill in yourself. Tanara can be translated in two ways. The first one is 'Tana Ra', which means: 'The Land of Ra' and Ra means Sun so we come up with 'Sunland'. The second way is: 'Tan-A-Ra'. The middle 'A' is able to be used for the word Tan as much as Ra so then we get; 'Tana Ara' which means 'Land of the snake' otherwise known as 'Snakeland'. The amusing fact of 'Snakeland' is that the genetic manipulation by Enki and Ninharsag took place in Africa. Scholars have come to agree that man was created in Africa and isn't it 'coincidental' then that so many areas in Africa have to do with snakes? Does this all stem from Enki's symbol, the two snakes? The same thought is given to the translation of Sahara. The Bedouin just translate it as 'red sand', otherwise known as 'the Red Country', but 'Sah' means sand, and 'Ara' means snake which creates the word 'Snakesand'. Snakes again. Throughout the whole world the ancient peoples talked about snakes and gods. That isn't just a fluke if you ask me. You could also ask yourself where the current day doctor's symbol; the staff of Aesculapius comes from. To me it seems logical that it is a reminder of the genetic interventions of the gods from Nibiru.

Vowels and consonants

Fascinated by the above it reminded me once again of the translations from the Milk Hill inscription, especially the word 'Chm'. This was especially due to the fact that there was something in the back of my mind that was not completely satisfied and I felt that I was overlooking something. The Tenere in Tanara story was still fresh in my mind so that evening I dropped by Ora's place. My question to her was simple.

'Can you fill the vowels in differently in the Hebrew language just as in the Egyptian language, just as with Tenere in Tanara?' Ora told me that this was indeed possible so I showed her how matters stood for me. Considering the word 'Chm' would not leave my thoughts and I still had a very strong intuitive feeling that there was much more to this inscription than we had been able to retrieve up until now I could not let it be.

'Chm' could indeed be written as Cham or Chem. Chem, Shem, Sem and Sjem are pretty well all the same and they mean god or name. The names of Noah's three sons, Shem, Ham, and Japheth all mean; 'warmth', 'purity' and 'god' or 'name'. Therefore Chem, Shem, Sem or Sjem all mean god or name. Somewhere in the back of my head a little bell started ringing louder and louder. In Alan Alford's book he covered in full details the mistake of translations that he discovered in the Bible. In Genesis 6:4 it says tha'...The Nephilim were on the Earth in those days - and also afterward - when the sons of God went to the daughters of men and had children by them. They were the heroes of old, men of renown. The last part should not read 'heroes of old' but instead it should read 'men of Shem'. Shem /Sem in fact means name, but Shem/Sem also means 'aircraft'. When I hear the word 'aircraft', the first thing that pops into my mind is rocket. Doesn't 'Cham' also mean warmth? Does a rocket not thrust out warmth?

The ultimate translation of the inscription at Milk Hill is reaching its completion. There are a few different complimentary translations possible that all point to the same conclusion. Namely that in the distant past Ea/Enki/Ptah interfered with the evolution of man by means of genetic manipulation. On ancient illustrations he was pictured with two snakes twisted around each other, these represent and come from the double helix from the human DNA chains according to Sitchin. The ultimate 'message' in the inscription, depending on whether you put an 'A' or 'E' in 'Chm' or just leave it as Cham, consists of the following piece of information; 'a new Breed of People, a new Breed of People from Cham (also known as Ham), or a New Breed of People from Chem! The translations of the first two possibilities are pretty straightforward. Only the last one could leave us with more information it could be saying 'a New Breed of People from the aircraft/ and Chem/Shem' that the gods of Nibiru were a new breed of people that came to Earth in an aircraft 270,183 BC. The inscription also informs us that we are descendants from the gods. The same aircraft that are known as 'Vimana's and 'heavenly carriages' are described in ancient writings. All these and previous translations relate to the one and only conclusion; that our creators are 'extraterrestrial'! Amongst other things these same extraterrestrials are responsible for the various crop circle formations on our Earth, two of which are the formations near Alton-Barnes: the inscription of 1991 and the Double Helix of 1996. Coincidence? I don't think so!

Numbers and Letters

Just after I thought I had researched everything possible as far as the Milk Hill inscription was concerned my eye fell on the Numerical value that Ora had given to me during her translation of the Hebrew letters. She had placed the numbers above the coinciding letters. The Numerical aspect is something very interesting, more so because it is already more than 9000 years old and was used by many ancient peoples.

The total of the numbers from the Hebrew letters from the inscription came to 2802. What does 2802 mean? I didn't know and after an afternoon of intense equation solving I could not reach a conclusion either until I remembered the calculations that Alan Alford used in his book. When he set up the new chronology it had to correspond with the Biblical timeline of Adam to Noah, the Sumerian and Babylonian kings and the gods from before the flood, as Manetho drew them. Alford tells us that he achieved this new chronology by taking certain ages from before the flood and dividing them by 100. After the flood the ages had to be divided by 50. Just as Alford did I multiplied 2802 by 100. The result was 280,200, an astonishing result mainly because

Crop Circles, Gods and their Secrets

according to Alford's calculations the gods had landed on Earth around 270,183 BC. A calculation that I had mentioned earlier that has lot of logic to it and 280,200 is in the vicinity of that number. For my peace of mind it just wasn't close enough. What is the meaning of the number 280,200? After some deep pondering I continued with further calculations and proceeded to do the following; 280,200 – 270,183 = 10,017. So there I sat with a value that didn't mean much more to me than 280,200. The only thing I could think of was that 4 x 10,017 could possible be the circumference of the Earth but that is 40,074.15588919 km, a difference of 6,155889191 km. Not a lot, but certainly not the answer I was looking for. Eureka!! After a lot of fretting and puzzling I had it figured out. At first I couldn't do anything with the number 10,017 until a certain moment when it all became very clear to me. The number had to be put into mirror image because that's where it had come from when it was deciphered from the inscription and it had to be calculated according to the ancient Sumerian sexagesimal system of numbers! This is how I achieved an inconceivable result but first let me give you an example of how the ancient Sumerians counted and calculated.

The Sexagesimal system of numbers

The Sumerians did not have the decimal system which we use today at their disposal but instead they had the sexagesimal system of numbers. If we have to write the number 2500 than we do that in the following manner:

$$\frac{1000 \quad 100 \quad 10 \quad 1}{2 \quad \quad 5 \quad \quad 0 \quad \; 0} = 2500$$

You then get a total of 2500. The Sumerians wrote 2500 as 4140.The Sumerian system of numbers achieved this in the following way:

$$\frac{3600 \quad 600 \quad 60 \quad 10 \quad 1}{- \quad \quad 4 \quad \quad 1 \quad \; 4 \quad \; 0} = 2500$$

At the units above 3600 we discover the following varieties; 36,000, 216,000, 2,160,000, and 12,960,000. The last number 12,960,000 is exactly 500 times the cycle of precession of 25,920 years. I will return to all these numbers and their significance in the chapter discussing 'Gematrian Numbers'.

When I took the number 10,017 and calculated it the Sumerian way the result was 3617. The orbit time of Nibiru is 3600 years. 3617 is very close to that but according to my calculations I believe that they represent the following; the 1 is the first planet in the direction of the Sun (Pluto) that the gods outside of our solar system come across and therefore the Earth is number 7. This is how the numbers 17 get a logical explanation. After an orbit of 3600 years the gods caught sight of the first planet which enabled them to direct their course to the 7th planet, Earth.

But this was still not the answer that I was hoping to find. As was mentioned before the number 10,017 had to be used in mirror image considering the inscription was also in mirror image. The result of the reflection was 71,001, which according to the Sumerian sexagesimal system of numbers has a final result of 25,801. This number represents, except for the 1, the exact number the Egyptians had figured out as the total precession cycle of the Earth - 25,800 days! But what about the...1? A 1 represents the beginning. Something new. That was indeed the case with the 'New Breed of People! But that wasn't the only thing that the 1 meant. If the numerical value of the Hebrew numbers had been 270,200 instead of 280,200 then the result of 270,200 – 270,183 would not have been 10,107 but 00,017. The ultimate difference would be 17 and the figure 270,200 is a rounding off of the number 270,183. But if that was the case I could have never used the mirror image of the 17 because with 71 I do not get any further not even with the sexagesimal system of numbers. Therefore it is logical to assume that the numerical result had to equal 10,017 because otherwise I would have never been able to associate it's link with the Sumerian sexagesimal system of numbers.

Crop Circles, Gods and their Secrets

JHWH, or Shem ha-meforash

A pleasant incidental of all these calculations is that you sometimes get really fun calculations. Calculations that you can 'coincidentally' combine with other numbers, which really do represent a meaning. Such was the case when I again examined the number 10,017. The total numerical value is 9 (1+0+0+1+7=9). The mirror image of the number gives us the exact same result, but when I separated the number 7, and the 2 (1+1) I got 72 (7+2=9). At first glance it seems as if you cannot accomplish anything with those results but pay attention to the outcome of these numbers and the literal translation of them.

According to the Cabalists the number 72 is equal to JHWH, later translated as Jehovah by the Bible translators. The Cabalists used a Tetragrammeton, for the unpronounceable Name of God, JHWH (see illustration).

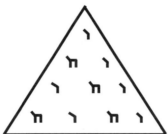

In ancient times when one still knew the proper pronunciation of the Holy Name it was only uttered once a year on the Day of Atonement. The wise men were only permitted to verbally pass the pronunciation down to their students once every seven years. Before that time he was known as 'Shem ha-meforasj', the 72 syllable name of God, consisting of 216 letters (2+1+6=.... 9!). The proper pronunciation of the unpronounceable Name of God has been lost over time taking into consideration that the Hebrew language (just as the Egyptian) does not have any vowels. When you figure out the name JHWH in the Tetragrammeton it corresponds with Shem ha-meforash. We presume that the name has the same force. The striking fact of the literal translation of Sjem ha-meforash is that it means; 'the Flying God'! Isn't that exactly what was said in the Milk Hill inscription, namely 'the New Breed of People from Shem'! The New Breed of People from the aircraft, in other words, The Flying Gods from Nibiru who descended to Earth around 270,183 BC.

Milk Hill – Thailand

Just as I thought I had translated everything from the Alton Barnes inscription I received a phone call from a good friend who told me that there was a picture of King Bhumibol Adulyadej of Thailand in the newspaper. At first sight Thailand has absolutely nothing to do with this book, let alone with the crop circles discussed by myself but after that telephone call I was forced to become engrossed by the history of Thailand because there were some very striking and pertinent facts in that particular article.

On the 5th of August 1999, King Bhumibol Adulyadej celebrated his birthday. The newspaper had published a beautiful coloured photograph of the King in full regalia underneath the golden canopy in his royal boat. The King navigated along the river Chao Phraya towards the Temple of the Rising Sun. With this the go-ahead was given for a month long party in honour of the 72nd birthday of the King of Thailand. The King of Thailand King Bhumibol Adulyadej has been reigning on his throne for 53 years making him the world's longest ruling monarch. During the trip through Bangkok to the Temple of the Rising Sun, the royal boat was accompanied by 52 decorated ships which were manned by 2082 rowers who were all decked out in traditional Siamese costumes.

At the moment that I saw the numbers in the newspaper article I felt as if I had been struck by lightning. 2082 Rowers! I knew this number because the mirror image of this number 2082 can be found in the numerical value of the Hebrew sentence that I was able to decipher and take from the Alton Barnes inscription. The numerical value of all the Hebrew letters in the message 'Sewet Chm Anasim Gadasim' is 2802 (the number 2802 was a number I had already been able to justify as 280,200 as you have previously read). Considering that this message was the mirrored version of the Alton Barnes inscription, the original version is 2082! Why does the King have 2082 rowers and not 2080 or 2090? Why was the King accompanied by 52 boats, why not more or less? Why was there such a big party when the King turned 72? Was the fact being celebrated that the King had now gone through and survived one complete degree of the precession cycle of the Earth? Do the 52 boats represent the number or the game of Thoth? To make it even crazier if one adds 2082 and 2802 together you get 4884 which are exactly the last four digits of my telephone number!! Coincidence or ...?

Further research has taught me that on the 6th of April 1782 General Chakri became the first King of the Chakri Dynasty. His official name was King Rama I. This dynasty still reigns today. The current King Bhumibol Adulyadej is the 9th King of the Chakri descendants and officially his name is Rama IX. King Bhumibol Adulyadej was born on the 12th of May 1927. The research was also able to provide me with information about Thailand itself and the most astonishing thing that I came across is that Thailand consists of 72 provinces.

In summary you could say that, using numerology, the birth date of the current King of Thailand can be converted to 9, he is actually called Rama 9, and the number of the provinces can be converted to 9. Furthermore King Bhumibol Adulyadej has a white parasol positioned above his throne and it is made up of 9 layers. Once again the number 9 can be found here. Could this all be purely coincidental? Would this be the same coincidence that I keep coming across in the various crop circle formations? Or as has been the case, is there more to it then simply numbers? I think so.

As for the explanation of the amount of rowers (2082) and the amount of boats (52) of King Bhumibol Adulyadej of Thailand I have to jump ahead somewhat to an area that still has to be covered about Teotihuacan, Mexico and what it is that Hugh Harleston Jr. discovered about this area. Just to be brief, Harleston discovered a unit of measurement in Teotihuacan of 1.05954 meters. Harleston also discovered that 1.05954 x 378 (another unit of measurement) x 100,000 = 40,049.58953 kilometres. According to Harleston this is quite an accurate account of the circumference of the Earth. This number instantly caught my eye because 2082 : 52 = 40.03846153846. If we move the decimal up three places then we get 40,038.46153846. The difference between 40,049.58935 and 40,038.46153846 is merely 11.12781154 kilometres. According to current day calculations the circumference of the Earth is 40,074.15588919 kilometres. The difference between the largest and the smallest number is merely 35 kilometres and that hasn't been calculated too badly by a civilisation that, according to the 'experts', lived in the stone age!

Crop circles and the proto-language

A little while ago I had my good friend Evert over for an evening visit. He was the person who had informed me of Sitchin's work several years ago. As usual it didn't take very long for our conversation to come round to the usual topics of UFOs, the 12th planet, ancient civilisation, Egypt and naturally of course crop circles. Evert has been absorbed with the research involving the proto-language, which he believes, is where all our current day languages stem from. He had notified me of these ideas several times already but personally I was not quite convinced. The evening progressed steadily and at a certain moment we got to the topic of his discoveries. He gave me a few examples of modern day words that he could convert by means of the protolanguage. I had to admit that there were a few remarkable findings amongst his theory and I decided to put it to the test, not only for my own benefit but also for his. I precisely wrote down all the letters of the Milk Hill inscription 'sewet chm anasim gadasim' in a row. To add a little spice to it I wrote the letters in mirror image so this is what he got to see; 'misadag misana mhc tewes'. Several days later he told me what it was that he had deciphered from this inscription. I stood perplexed. He had succeeded, by means of a self-taught system, which he calls the 'proto-language of all languages', to decipher the inscription. After I read his 'translation' I decided to tell him that I had written the numbers down in mirror image. He also translated the normal version and once again there was an astounding outcome. The mirror image findings resulted in the following; 'seeing less due to adjustments in our DNA. Knowledge was living. I saw deeds'. Once again I want to impress upon you that he really did not know what I had given him. He didn't have a clue as to what I meant with the letters that I had given to him. The normal version was translated as the following; 'the knowledge that comes from afar has been placed in the body (in the DNA), guaranteed for always. Brought in (in the DNA) and formed in the waters (bodily fluids). Guaranteed intellectual energy that has been brought in.'

Inconceivable!By means of the method developed by him, indeed using somewhat different wording, he had described the same thing from the inscription and the DNA formation as I had by means of my own decoding system. In my opinion the translation is imperceptibly close to that which Sitchin translated from the ancient Sumerian clay tablets. Being able to see less refers to the fact that at one point the gods genetically intervened. The Popol Vuh, the holy book of the ancient Quiche Mayans of Guatemala and Mexico, tells us about being able to see less. As I told you earlier several gods were quite perturbed with the fact that mankind could 'see and know' as much as the gods themselves. With that in mind it was decided that 'mist' should be blown into their eyes to limit the 'seeing' and 'knowledge'. The ability of the gods to genetically manipulate had come to be a reality. The first people were actually walking around! The 'I saw deeds' could be referring to the gods who saw mankind performing 'deeds', but this is only my own interpretation. The translation of the original version speaks for itself. The gods came from afar and indeed they placed the guaranteed knowledge for always in our DNA. The rest of the translation goes without saying because the waters (bodily fluids) could be referring to a test tube or a womb. The gods have guaranteed ability in mankind, a guaranteed ability to reproduce the genetically adapted human because the forerunner of the first human, the LU.LU, was not able to reproduce.

1991/2000

Nine years after the appearance of the inscription at Milk Hill, Wiltshire and more than six months of research, calculations and heavy thought have brought us to the previously mentioned results. What appeared to be a simple crop circle formation at first sight turns out to have a complex complete history of man concealed within it. It was quite a job to research all the data, calculate and control the facts but boy was it worth it. Without the 'coincidental' chain of events that led me to this point there would have never been a solution to this inscription. Incidentally the word 'coincidence' does not exist in my vocabulary.

A nice addition to the Milk Hill inscription is the following; just a little while ago I received an email address from the I.C.C.A. in Germany. The abbreviation stands for International Crop Circle Archive. The director, Andreas Müller is currently occupied with charting all the crop circle formation statistics. As curious as I am, I asked him if he had any more information regarding the Milk Hill inscription and the DNA spiral. After a while I received a small notice, which contained the following information:

"Gerald Hawkins, a famous American astronomer also researched the Milk Hill inscription. He did this together with a team of twelve language experts and a special linguistic computer program. The computer program was capable of making 18,000 variations in 42 different languages. Hawkins went on to say that the inscription consisted of 6 different letters. There were three possibilities of which the final result was a Latin text, which said; 'OPPONO ASTOS'. Hawkins further translation of that quote was; 'I m against works of confusion' or, more literally, 'I am against hoaxers'."

From that you can conclude that the 'crop circle formation creators' are not pleased with the people who are reproducing them. The serious crop circle formation researcher is also annoyed with this fact since it interferes with his or her research. The reason that the true 'crop circle formation creators' are not happy with the imitation formations could very well lie in the idea that I had suggested before namely that in a 'fake formation' one could easily be creating a negative message (see section on Crop Circles, the 7 Seals).

Crop circles, gods, pyramids and DNA

Until thus far my crop circle formation research has proven that there are various devas (Sanskrit for deity) responsible for the various worldwide crop circle formations. For my taste, 'diva' is too vague of a word so I went on to see if I could give these divas a name in order to clarify some things. If you want proof of this you can see it in the inscription at Milk Hill. We wonder what else these divas, also known as gods, have done? Where did they live and what did they do? Besides various constructions in South and Central-America the pyramids of Egypt are the most mysterious constructions that 'they' ever built. From here we will take a little trip to the ancient Egypt of the gods.

3 The origin of the Great Pyramid

Pyramids, what is the truth?

There have been so many truths and lies written about the famous pyramids of Giza, Egypt, which have been continuously researched. After centuries of research and speculations one is still not in agreement over who, what, when and how the Great Pyramid has been built. Modern day Egyptologists are in agreement that Khufu was the builder of the Great Pyramid. Khufu is his Egyptian name and Cheops is the Greek rendition of the name. The lady and gentleman Egyptologists are certain that there is no possible doubt concerning the 'fact' that above the King's Chamber in the so called 'decompression chamber' a cartouche was found with Khufu's name written on it. According to the Egyptologists this is the most convincing piece of evidence that Khufu/Cheops built the Great Pyramid. Ever since the 'discovery' of the cartouche of Khufu by Colonel Howard Vyse in 1837 its origin has been contested. Quite soon after his 'discovery' someone thought that he had possibly painted the cartouche in a highly ambiguous location himself. After some very thorough research Zecharia Sitchin was able to produce enough evidence in 1980 that the cartouche was an imitation. Sitchin tells us that the cartouche was painted with symbols that weren't used for another 2000 years after those that Khufu used. Even though there is evidence against it many Egyptologists still accept that this cartouche is the convincing evidence that Khufu was the builder of the Great Pyramid of Giza.

But does the Egyptologists' opinion, which attributes the pyramids to different Egyptian pharaohs, still stand? Are we to believe that a pyramid is simply nothing more than a burial chamber for a deceased pharaoh? What are the pyramids telling us, especially the Great Pyramid of Giza? Let us look at this whole issue from a totally different perspective than has ever been used before. There are various convictions as far as the Great Pyramid of Giza is concerned. The one

Crop Circles, Gods and their Secrets

thing that all these opinions have in common is that ...not one of them is being recognised by present day Egyptologists. We then ask ourselves why these beliefs are not shared? Once a certain topic has your interest and you further involve yourself into the subject you logically start to form an opinion on the matter. The opinion is based on what you have learned. What surprises me the most, and then perhaps on the other hand not, is the fact that the Egyptologists are absolutely convinced of their story which is patently based on quicksand. Why would one do that?

Imagine the following; you are interested in something. You go to school to study that particular subject. You then proceed according to the guidelines of the teachings. These teachings allow no room for other possible convictions so you are stuck in the same pattern. After years and years of being locked in the same pattern it is very difficult to sway from the taught methods and what at that time seemed to be the correct pattern. What could possibly be more difficult than a 'scholar' having to admit to an unschooled person that he is wrong and that the unschooled person is able to see the truths for what they are better than the person who studied for it? Well, heavens forbid the possibility of an unschooled person being able to solve a mystery by plain logical thinking when an Egyptologist has never thought of these options or better yet; has never wanted to think of these possibilities. When discoveries are ridiculed and denied such as those that Bauval did, then it is the Egyptologists who bring forth their accepted knowledge as the 'truth'. Unfortunately the knowledge which has been brought out in the open regarding the Great Pyramid at Giza is based on nothing but quicksand. But let us look at the following; the Egyptologists consequently wipe the ancient written facts from the table because they prove the opposite of what they have been trying to convince the public of all these years.

What do the Arab legends tell us?

It is very difficult to deny the fact that the Egyptians have never built a pyramid. Around 3000 BC people started to try to reproduce the Great Pyramid at Giza. The Step Pyramid at Dahshur, belonging to Pharaoh Djoser is most likely the oldest pyramid built by the Egyptians. The reason I say "most likely", is because of the fact that there is still around eighty percent more still hidden than what has been excavated so far,buried under the desert sand. In days long gone by, it is said that that there was once a white outer shell on

Crop Circles, Gods and their Secrets

the Great Pyramid. Old Arab traditions and legends also tell of this white outer shell. With a white outside layer like that the outside of the pyramid would look completely even and white.

This outside layer disappeared during the large earthquake of 1301 AD. The inhabitants of Cairo used the stone blocks to rebuild the city. To be able to determine the reason as to the loss of the outer layer we have to look back another 500 years previous when Harun Al Rashid awarded Egypt to his son caliph Abdullah Al-Mahmun in the year 827 AD Harun Al-Rashid had already taken over North-Africa in the name of the Holy War, the Jihad, to convert all the inhabitants of those regions to Islam. Al-Mahmun thought 'I am the boss and Egypt is mine, the Pyramid is mine and I'm going to see what is buried in it' especially since he had heard the old legends of gold weapons that did not rust and glass that could bend without breaking. Al-Mahmun chopped a hole in the outer layer and went on a exploratory tour. It is most probable that this would have caused the whole outer layer to disconnect during the earthquake of 1301 AD After the Earthquake the surviving inhabitants of Cairo used the white layer to rebuild their city and homes. The ancient Egyptians used to call Cairo 'On' and the Arabians called it 'El Kahire', which means 'the great victory'.

The same legends tell us that on the outside white layer there were various written texts. The question is: what exactly was written there? Around 1200 AD, Dr. Abu Sahyd had his practice across from the Great Pyramid. He spent most of his free time on his greatest passion and hobby: the Egyptian antiquity. He most likely had the texts on the Great Pyramid, which he wasn't able to decipher himself, translated by the Copts, who lived in Athkaptah. Athkaptah means Second Heart of Ptah, which is what Egypt is. Kaptah is Heart of Ptah and that was Atlantis. The Copts were the only ones who at that time had mastered and were able to read ancient Egyptian hieroglyphics.

According to Abu Sahyd one of the most striking texts was that the great pyramid was built in 'falling Vulture in Cancer (zodiac sign)'. Arabic traditions and writings do not share the Egyptologists accomplished answer that was derived at simply due to availability, so therefore no attention is paid to the 'falling Vulture in Cancer (zodiac)'. (In Mexico the same phenomenon is known as 'the falling Eagle in Cancer'.) One just leaves it laying on the wayside mainly because no one knows the meaning of this phrase. Vulture stands for Sun, and that is how 'falling Vulture in Cancer' signifies the falling of the Sun. On first thought a falling Sun sounds just as ridiculous as a falling Vulture, but if we look at it more closely it really isn't that crazy.

Was the Great Pyramid built in the period of Cancer?

The Sun is always ahead in the zodiac except in the springtime, when the Sun runs behind, as if it were 'falling'. To summarise the ancient pyramid texts, it says the pyramids are built in 'falling Vulture in Cancer'. If we translate this into plain English then it says that the pyramid was built when the Sun lowered into the springtime in the period of cancer, which ran from approx. 8810 – 6650 BC. Therefore the Great Pyramid is minimally 8650 to 10,810 years old!

But if this is true than how do Robert Bauval's calculations work? By means of a computer program his calculations have shown that together with the river Nile the pyramid complex is an exact mirror image of the constellation of Orion and the Milky Way around 10,450 BC. Bauval also calculated that at that exact time 10,450 BC, Orion showed up in the zodiac sign of Leo and that is why the Sphinx was looking at the constellation of Leo. According to Bauval the Sphinx was originally a lion but I seriously have my doubts considering there are more Sphinxes. There are several avenues of sphinxes with 150 sphinxes on opposite sides all representing the body of a lion and with the head of the pharaoh of that time or with the head of the zodiacal constellation Aries - the ram. The lion was the royal sign of the leader, the Pharaoh. The age of Leo ran from ca. 10,970 until 8810 BC. Did the builders of the Great Pyramid make a mistake as to when it was built? Were they so busy building the pyramid that they did not remember in which year or zodiacal constellation they were dwelling? Was Bauval so incredibly far off with his approximations that we had just better trash his information?

Old Arabian legends go on to tell us that the pyramids were built to retain the knowledge until after the great flood. Before the flood the gods had given the humans an awful lot of information and the humans pleaded with the gods to be allowed to retain that wisdom until after the flood. So which calculation is the correct one? If we use the 10,450 BC which Bauval used, then we do not reach an agreement with the 'falling Vulture in Cancer', because Cancer comes after Leo. Could the Great Pyramid possibly be from before the great flood and how would you figure that out? Let us examine the ancient Arabic legends more closely and see if we can gain more information from them.

Is the Great Pyramid older than 10,450 BC?

10,468 BC is the correct date that has been accepted by the scholars as the last date of a polar shift. The second to last pole-shift was in

± 24,000 BC. During a pole-shift the magnetic north and magnetic south exchange poles with each other. The + and − poles change as the Earth, the Sun and the middle of the Milky Way are in a straight line. It doesn't always occur at a 'set' time, as long as the Earth is not in a 'phase' when it is in the straight line. If the centre of the Milky Way, which is a black hole, sends out a − on the 'top side' and the Earth has a + there, then we can speak of a polar reversal of the magnetic poles. The ancient Egyptians told the Greek historian Herodotus that this had already happened 4 times before. Everybody talks about Herodotus, but the most important statement that the Sun has risen four times outside of its normal place is something that is forgotten. Mainly because this isn't possible so therefore it is labelled as nonsense or as a misunderstood phenomenon. Just suppose the Sun really did not rise four times in the normal place, that is to say twice where the Sun sets and twice where the Sun rises. If you spread your fingers then you can see the four Suns that Herodotus is talking about in between your fingers. The fingers equal five periods of time. Did the Mayans on the other side of the Atlantic Ocean not have something similar? They divided their precession cycle into five periods of 5200 years. Only the Egyptians speak of five periods of 13,000 years, which gives a total of 65,000 years! We have just seen that approximately once every 13,000 years a shift of the magnetic poles occurs. I have often discussed the possibility of a geological shift when there is a magnetic pole shift. It is very well possible that with the last shifts the Earth turned completely. So in other words the North Pole exchanged with the South Pole. The whole Earth was 'hanging upside down' before the great flood. There are also several other opinions that tell us that for unknown reasons the Earth turned opposite to that which it does today. In both cases the end result is the same, that the Sun would not rise in her normal place. I am not completely convinced with this theory considering I came across some more information written by the ancient Arabic chronicle writers who noted that '… the reason Saurid had the Great Pyramid built was because he had a dream, 300 years before the devastating great flood, that the Earth turned, the people sought refuge and the stars came tumbling down'.

Crop Circles, Gods and their Secrets

Further along we see that Saurid was one of Thoth's names. Other ancient writers such as Al Makir, Ibn Batuta, Watwati, Makrimi and Sorar all share the same story and that is that Hermes/Saurid built the Great Pyramid in order to save the knowledge during 'the great flooding'.

If we would take the text from the pyramid that was translated by Abu Sahyd and compare them to the 'falling Vulture in Cancer' then I really feel that this text becomes a lot clearer. If the Earth actually 'hung' upside down before the great flood then the Earth retains her regular rotation around the Earth's axle. The only difference being (besides, Earthquakes, volcanic eruptions and so on) that the Sun rises in the west. If the Sun rises in the west it also means that the zodiac rotates the other way and that before the time period of Leo there is Cancer! The 'falling Vulture in Cancer' therefore gets a whole different meaning. It means that before the time period Leo there was a time period of Cancer that ran from approximately 13,130 until 10,970 BC. So if the Great Pyramid was built in the time of Cancer which comes before Leo then it means that the Great Pyramid is actually ca. 15,000 years old, older than had been thought up until now!

What is it then that Bauval discovered?

If the Great Pyramid was built around ca. 13,000 BC then what does the time period of 10,450 BC that Bauval mentions signify? According to Bauval's calculations the three pyramids along the Nile are an exact copy of the zodiacal constellation Orion and the Milky Way around 10,450 BC. This date merely indicates a large radical change. Around that time the Leo time period started (ca. 10,970 / 8810 BC), in which time the great flood also took place. Nothing more and nothing less. In his book 'Gods from the Cosmos' Alan Alford thoroughly calculated the time of the great flood to be 10,983 BC. The difference between both calculations is only 13 years. The question still remains as to what is so significant about the date that Bauval discovered?

According to Drunvalo Melchizedek, Thoth built the Great Pyramid to preserve the knowledge and wisdom of many things, one of them being Atlantis, to survive the great flood. Egyptologists tell us that it is Chephren who built the Great Pyramid especially considering it was the name 'Chephren' which was found carved into the walls. Chephren was one of the five names that an Egyptian King such as Cheops had. The strangest part of all this is that Chephren is also one of the names given to Thoth! According to my idea Thoth, who is known by different names all over the world, is the only god who has buried a lot of knowledge under the ground. The reason I say this is because if you believe those involved then there is a twelve-story building that has been found underneath the Great Pyramid. It is rumoured that there is a complete city under there! Drunvalo Melchizedek also speaks of the 'Brotherhood of Tat of immortal souls who lived in the underground city under the Giza complex'. Tat was a son of Thoth. The names of Thoth which I know of so far (see illustration) are amongst others; Ningisjzidda, Mercury, Hermes, Taautus, Quetzalcoatl, Viracocha and Kukulcan. Other sources of information mention Thoth under the names of Henoch, Saurid, Idris. In Atlantis Thoth's names was Chiquitet Arlich Vomalites. No doubt there are other names such as Tehuti, but the above-mentioned names are the most important renditions.

Thoth

According to my idea the reason that the Pyramids and the Giza complex are positioned exactly as the starry skies around 10,450 BC is as follows. If you have hidden 'something' that you don't want anyone else to know about what do you do? You expose the future human race to a mystery. They will search high and low to try to figure out what could possibly be the meaning of the Great Pyramid and its complex. They will come up with various possibilities and think of utterly ridiculous theories just to try to justify what the whole complex could represent. For years they will be so occupied with 'The Mystery of the Great Pyramid' that the eye will not be able to see farther than what is right in front of their noses. But in the end, when the time is right and mankind is ready, the secrets shall be revealed. This is what I feel was Thoth's purpose in building the Great Pyramid of Giza.

Twelve strands of DNA?

The question that arises is then what is it that we are not supposed to know yet? Mankind now has two strands of DNA. Formerly this was different. We then possessed a twelve strand DNA but through the gods doing by means of genetic manipulation in our DNA we now possess merely two strands.

Popol Vuh, the holy book of the ancient Quiche Mayans of Guatemala and Mexico, tell us the same story. This book tells us that the ancestors of the Mayans 'were gifted with such an intellect that they could see very far'. Several gods were troubled by the fact that humans could 'see, hear and know' as much as some of the gods themselves and therefore questioned if it was necessary for the humans to know as much as their creators. Discussions were carried out and the gods came to the agreement that the humans 'would have mist blown into their eyes to limit their eyesight', as well as limiting their 'knowledge'. Doesn't the Popol Vuh tell us here of the story of genetic manipulation performed by the gods? First mankind was equal to the gods but due to procedures 'sight and knowledge' were changed. Was mankind set back to a two-strand DNA from a very complex twelve-strand DNA? Would a twelve-strand DNA take care that we would be able to 'see and know' as much as the gods in ancient times again?

If we could possess a twelve-strand DNA then we would be able to have multidimensional experiences. In my eyes Drunvalo Melchizedek's perfect pronouncement would have more meaning to it now than we have allowed it to have, namely 'We are not human beings with spiritual experiences but spiritual beings with human experiences'!

The question arises as to what it is that keeps us in the two-strand DNA? During my quest for answers I discovered that there is 'something' hidden underneath the Great Pyramid that keeps mankind in its two-strand DNA state. According to my theory it is something that the gods brought down to the Earth to keep man in his twostrand DNA. The Popol Vuh tells us the story of how and why. Therefore you could say that if the 'something' that was buried by the gods were to be found again that mankind would have the twelve-strand DNA at its disposal! Man would once again possess the senses that were manipulated away. This would represent the 'knowledge, seeing and hearing' of things that we currently cannot see, hear or know. This knowledge has currently been put aside for psychics, mediums and the paranormal only. We are becoming the spiritual beings that we actually should be. The only problem being is that if we were to get the full dose of DNA returned to us all at once the largest part of the Earth's population would not survive this phenomenon. It will have to be a very gradual process if we want to survive this transaction. I feel that we are already being prepared bit by bit as to what is going to happen. Crop circle formations are a part of this. It is a striking fact that over the years there has been an increase of movies exposing us to aliens, comet strikes, and total devastation. Are we being prepared in this manner as to what is going to happen? If this is so, are there yet more secrets being kept from the ordinary person?

Ancient myths and legends have spoken about the fact that the world has gone under various times already but that the world has been 'reborn' on each of these occasions. Is the same fate waiting upon us? Will we go on in a new world or is a large disaster hanging over our heads and will most of the population not survive it? That could possibly be looking too far into the future but we must not forget the traditions and legends of the ancient peoples. Will we be ruined or is there a possibility that we will go on into another dimension? A dimension where mankind could return to the twelve-strands of DNA that we once possessed in days long past?

Why was the Great Pyramid built?

Even though this question really isn't very easy to answer I will give it a genuine try especially considering the fact that during my quest I came across various 'strange' facts that I do not want to withhold from the reader. As I mentioned earlier I discovered that Thoth built the Great Pyramid around 14,000 BC. My question is why was the Great Pyramid built exactly where it was and not at a different location. Why not a few kilometres to the south or to the left? And with what purpose has this 'wonder of the world' been built here?

Certainly one of the strangest things that I have come across is the fact that the Great Pyramid has been built at this exact location to let the human race, who survived the great flood, be under the influence of the right cosmic rays that they would need. This all sounds a bit odd at first. I thought this too but when you discover that there is more to this than meets the eye it doesn't take you very long to come to the conclusion that 'something' very complicated is at work here and that everything is going along according to a preordained plan. The person who is responsible for this could very well be that person with a capital G. The Great Pyramid of Giza is standing exactly where it was built thousands of years ago. The purpose of it was and is multifunctional. It served as a beacon for the approach route of the Anunnaki. It is also known that ancient Egyptian priests held initiations there. These initiations were completed after the initiate had spent some time lying in the 'sarcophagus' in the King's chamber. The initiate had then been inaugurated into the world of cosmic knowledge. One of the main reasons that the Pyramid has been built for is the following reason. As I mentioned earlier the Great Pyramid was built to let mankind receive the correct cosmic influence. This cosmic absorption is necessary to be able to go one step further in our development as 'spiritual beings with human experiences'. In truth we are actually being helped from the outside.

Before the great flood the Earth stood upside down. In other words the North Pole was at the South Pole and the South Pole was at the North Pole. During the magnetic and geological reversal of the poles approximately 13,000 years ago the Earth did not return to its' original stance. The Earth remained at an angle. As we read earlier this hanging at an angle is known as an inclination. This inclination amounts to 23.5 degrees. The imaginary circle that the inclined Earth's axis traces in the heavens amounts to 25,920 years. This movement of the equinoxes along the ecliptic plane is called the precession of the equinoxes. Amongst other things the Great Pyramid has been built as an acupuncture pressure point for the Earth. It sounds a bit odd but please continue to pay attention. Imagine a little ball of styrofoam. If you were to put a pin or a needle into the ball then by the power of a magnet you could manipulate this ball any which way you choose without ever touching it with your hands. You could hang the magnet up somewhere and therefore place the little styrofoam ball any which way you want. The exact same thing happened to the Earth. Thoth's enormous cosmic knowledge was responsible for the fact that after the reversal of the poles the Earth never returned to its 'upright position' but remained at an inclination of 23.5 degrees. Only at this angle can the cosmic influence go to work. The reasoning behind this might be incomprehensible but at the same time logical which can be concluded from the following bit of information.

Breathing and the precession cycle

Man breathes an average of 18 breaths per minute. If you multiply 18 times by 60 minutes times 24 hours then you get a total of 25,920 respirations per 24 hours. What an odd number you say. Well no, have we not come across this number previously when we spoke of the precession cycle of the Earth? Our body still harbours a number that the Earth has impressed in it since the great flood. Namely the 23.5 degrees that the Earth's axis is out of plumb. The human body's heart is out of line with the imaginary axle of the Earth. The degree at which the heart is angled amounts to 23.5 degrees! Strange? Not at all because only in this way are we granted the privilege to receive all the cosmic influence that we are given at this moment. It is our choice as to what we choose to do with this information. Mankind and the Earth have become one since the great flood. Since that time we have been in evolution. This is not as a result from direct assistance from the gods of Nibiru. These days there are several developments underway. In my opinion we are being helped from outside forces to return mankind into the twelve-strands of DNA that we once possessed. An example of this is the crop circle that was found on the 26th of June 1999 on Allington Down, Wiltshire, England. The formation was named the triple DNA strand (see photograph).

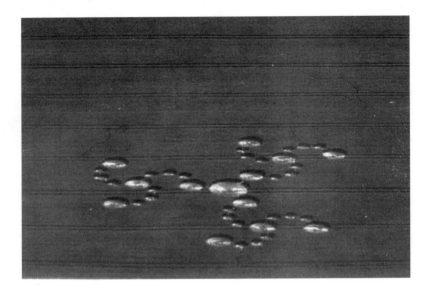

In my opinion this is the first step towards a twelve-strand DNA which was taken away from us in the past by the Anunnaki. It wouldn't suprise me at all that in the coming years more crop circles will be found that have the shape of a quadruple, quintuple or sextuple DNA strand. According to my theories the crowning piece will be a twelve-strand DNA crop circle formation. During my research I have already come across the fact of an altered DNA. There are people walking around already with an altered DNA. The blood of these people is no longer the same as it was before. Therefore I wasn't surprised to find out either that according to Drunvalo Melchizedek there are already people and children that have an altered DNA. According to Drunvalo one percent of the world's population already has an altered DNA, which equates to approximately sixty million people. The 'something' which is responsible for keeping mankind in the two-strand DNA, which is buried underneath or close to the Great Pyramid, has almost been resolved and then we will be able to progress one step higher. We are no longer stuck in the two strands of DNA into which our creators had locked us. But what is

Crop Circles, Gods and their Secrets

that 'something' which is buried under the plateau of Giza? I will explain in the section '52, the game of Thoth'.

Were the ancient peoples insane?

In summary you could suppose that in earlier times people were not crazy. Actually the opposite can be concluded because Arabian traditions tell us that the Great Pyramid was built to retain the knowledge until after the great flood. Drunvalo tells us that Thoth 'spoke' to him and told him that he (Thoth) was the one who built the Great Pyramid shortly after 14,000 BC for the above mentioned purpose and for other things. For the rest there is still the 'Falling Vulture in Cancer'. All this information equates to a period of 13,000 to 13,500 BC. That is more than 15,000 years ago and ample time before the great flood. And why not? We think that with our advanced learning, technology and scientific knowledge that we know everything while in actual fact we know hardly anything at all. We assume that everything has to be based and proven by a scientific theory whilst, if we were just to base it on old myths and traditions as astonishing as they sometimes seem, I feel we would be a lot further ahead. If we could just go with the flow and not be so focused on learned knowledge and scientific titles. Do you really believe that our fore fathers all over the world had nothing better to do all day than make up stories about gods, aircraft, snakes and who knows what else? If we could just drop that train of thought for a while then we would accomplish a whole lot more than we have up until now. Why would the people of ancient times make up 'fables' just to make fools out of the future residents of mother Earth around the year 2000 AD? I don't think so because in every story there is a grain of truth, however odd it may seem in these modern times.

Logic, the key to everything

Muhammad ben Abdallah ben Abd el-Hakam gives us a very simple and very logical explanation as to why we know that the Great Pyramid is from before the great flood. That simply being the fact that if it were from after the great flood mankind would know a whole lot more about it today. In my opinion there isn't anything that can be brought up to oppose this verdict even though many a man would like to.

To the ancient Egyptians, Henoch was the builder of the Great Pyramid as the geographer Taki ad-Din Ahmad ben Ali ben Abd al Kadir ben Muhammad al-Makrizi (1364-1442) wrote in his Hitat. He mentioned that Henoch was known amongst the people of the world by four names; as Saurid, Hermes, Idris and Henoch. The passage in the Hitat that concerns this is in chapter 33 and goes as follows; '...the first Hermes, who in his capacities as a prophet, king and wiseman was called the Triplicate, read in the stars that a great flood would come. This is why he had the Pyramids built to bury the treasures, the writings of the scholars and everything that should not be lost or disappear, to protect all those precious things and to save them, thus my translation.

The question that arises immediately in the reader's mind is then why have none of these transcripts ever been found? This is because after Al Mahum chopped a hole into the wall of the Pyramid and looted it, evidence he never shared with the rest of the world as to what it was that he took out of the Great Pyramid. This comes as no surprise considering the fact that if someone won the main prize in a lottery they would not broadcast the news either. Al Mahum did the same and kept his mouth tightly shut. The golden harness and other golden things were melted down and used to pay the soldiers off with. The mummy that was in the golden harness was thrown away because at that time it had no value. For the rest I think that there is a portion hidden under the Great Pyramid and that not all the rooms in the Pyramid have been uncovered as of yet.

13,000 years ago

As mentioned earlier Thoth built the Great Pyramid to be able to survive the great flood and to save all the knowledge for mankind after the flood. What else was going on around the time of 11,000 BC? What follows is a portion of the many events that occurred at that time.

In the distant past various disasters have occurred where many animals became extinct, masses of land submerged under water and other landmasses arose. There were simply too many things that happened around that date. Mammoths were found, in the permafrost of Siberia, with undigested leftovers of plants in their stomachs that were never even growing there at that time.

The end of the last ice age is around 11,000 BC, with its peak being around 16,000 BC. The first recorded accounts of Atlantis, which is said to have been engulfed by the ocean around 11,000 BC as a result of various devastation's, appear in Timaeus and Critias, two dialogues by Greek philosopher Plato (these date back to the fifth century BC).

La Brea, USA

In May of 1995 I was on a 14-day holiday in California, USA. After having seen the usual tourist attractions such as Hollywood, Las Vegas and the Grand Canyon I took advantage of the situation to visit the 'George C. Page Museum of La Brea Discoveries' in Los Angeles. On the property outside of the museum there are these so called tar pits. They are under ground oil deposits that have pushed oil to the surface of the Earth through cracks. These tar pits are more than ten thousand years old. In prehistoric times these tar pits were covered with a layer of water. The animals that lived in that area at that time such as the sabre -tooth tiger, mammoth, deer, horses and even camels, came there to quench their thirst from that water. The daredevils or rather the more unfortunate of those animals walked into the treacherous water. Once they were standing in the water they became stuck and there was no way out. The tar was sticky and sucked the animals under like quicksand. Most of the animals that have been found in these tar pits are between 10,000 and 40,000 years old. The tar has preserved the skeletons of these many animals very well. Besides the various animals many plants, pollens, wood, leaves, insects, spiders, frogs etc have been found there.

Human remains have also been found there. We are speaking of the skeleton of a woman who fell into the tar about 9000 years ago. The woman named the 'La Brea Woman' was approximately 1.45 meters tall and between twenty and twent-five years old. It was impressive to be able to admire something so old just as all the aancient animals that were being exhibited there. The animals that were found there, are not the animals one would expect to find in the western part of the United States of America. Nowadays they are no longer there. Why not?

While drilling into the ice cap in Greenland several years ago researchers discovered that the air temperature that had been stable all these years had suddenly risen on average by 5°C. This all happened in a time frame of between three to ten years.

Many animal types became extinct. This was a great disaster and it happened approximately 10,500 BC, when the South Pole of the Earth became the North Pole of the Earth and the great flood threw the rest of mankind into great havoc. The face of the Earth no longer looked the same as before. We have been able to see that the cause of this could perhaps be a coincidence. The passage of Nibiru, an unstable icecap and the shifting of the Earth's crust such as the one Hapgood explains in his theory. In my opinion all these occurrences are due to Nibiru's passage. It just had to be that way. An end of a period in which the people of Atlantis had spoiled the whole lot by their high level technology. We are now on the same road of self-destruction just as the people of Atlantis. As it looks now we have not learned anything either and are about to enter a similar period.

Crop Circles, Gods and their Secrets

4 Return of the Gods

Planetary system with a message?

Although the crop circles seem to have been fairly simple in the early years, they have become more complex on a yearly basis. It seems as if the 'artists' of the formations selected a different theme every year to guide mankind. There were also certain formations from which one could decipher a kind of solar system. It seems that the purpose of the 'crop circle makers' is to clarify to us in which direction we should be searching or to portray to us as to where 'they' came from. In a few different pictograms, which could easily represent a solar system, it seems as if the orbits of different planets have been reproduced. You could therefore propose that the 'makers' of the pictogram want to show us where they come from or what we should look out for. On June 25 1995 a pictogram appeared outside of Winchester, Hampshire that looks very much like our own solar system complete with a few orbits (see photograph).

You can consider the Sun the centre point and the orbits around it are Mercury, Venus, Earth and Mars. The outside ring is the asteroid belt. Only the third orbit is empty, that is the one that belongs to the Earth, and it is empty. This could possibly be telling us that in the future there will be a solar system without the Earth and that the other planets will also be in the next dimension and that we do not belong to that as of yet. It is also possible that it depicts the view from Earth, of the planetary orbits. After all, the only planet missing from the night sky, is the one you are standing on!

52 + 13 = 65 circles

Interesting data is the fact that the 'asteroid belt' in the above mentioned formation consists of 65 circles, 52 clockwise, and 13 anti-clockwise. The numbers 52 and 13 were familiar to me because the Mayans also knew these two numbers. For the Mayans thirteen was a holy and important number, it exerts the motion of time; 13 (Tones) times 20 (Sun seals) makes a Tzolkin of 260 days (otherwise known as 260 Kin). There are also 13 Moons per year with 28 days per Moon cycle; together making 364 days (plus one day outside of the time). The Tzolkin is divided into 5 castles of 52 days each, but also into 4 seasons each 65 days long, both are again divisible by 13, and 52 + 13 = 65.

The Tzolkin of 260 Kin is, amongst other things, one of the smallest impressions (dimension) in proportion to the precession cycle of almost 26000 years. All the planets of our solar system actually rotate in a flat plane around the Sun. However the Earth does not stand upright with regard to facing the Sun. The Earth's imaginary axis that runs through the North and South Pole actually stands at a bit of an angle. These are known as the magnetic North and South Poles. This angle, which is at 23.5 degrees, is known as the inclination. The tilting Earth axis scribes a circle in the sky, when the two planes make a complete revolution with respect to each other. This movement of the equinoxes along the ecliptic is

Crop Circles, Gods and their Secrets

called the precession of the equinoxes; this is what is known as a precession cycle. You can get the same effect from the wobble of a spinning top, as it is just about to topple over. The top of the top scribes a circle. This precession cycle which amounts to 25,920 years has been divided into 12 equal pieces of 2160 years by astrologers and astronomers. When the Earth has made a complete circle in the heavens then a complete cycle of 25,920 years has passed.

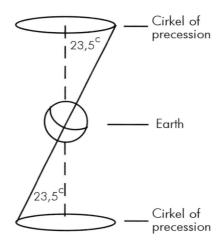

The Sumerians and the Egyptians already knew of the Precession cycle and the accompanying 12 Zodiacal signs. The Sumerians divided the Precession cycle by 12x2160 =25,920 years while the Egyptians counted 2150 per constellation and came to a total of 25,800 years for a Precession cycle. These calculations of 25,920 and 25,800 years are a mathematical approximation. Current estimates have shown that a Precession cycle takes approximately 25,776 years, which is 12 x 2148 years.

The Mayans divided this time into five divisions of 5200 years. These divisions were known as The Great Count. A Great Count (the current one is running from 3114 BC until the 21st of December 2012) was then divided into 13 Baktuns of 144,000 days each etc.

In summary:
If you combine the wheel of 260 days (Tzolkin) with the wheel of 365 days (known as 'the Haab') then you get a clockwork of 18,980 days, and that is precisely 52 years! There are 4 large seasons that continue on for 13 years. In the Western world we are familiar with the Gregorian calendar and we add 1 day to our calendar every leap year (every 4 years). The Mayans, the Aztecs and the Toltecs had 13 leap days every 52 years, which comes to the same end result as in Western civilisation.

In combination with the Sun, Moon and Venus years they could calculate a cycle of 52 years. Venus was an important star, which was known by Central Americans as the deliverer of culture, knowledge and many other things, and his name was Quetzalcoatl. The Mayans knew him as Kukulcan, and the Egyptians name for Kukulcan is....Thoth. Thoth was associated with the magical number 52. In Egypt Thoth had 'the game of 52, in which no mortal would survive'. The sides of the Great Pyramid of Giza, which were built by Thoth, have an inclination angle of 52 degrees. Later on I will return to the number 52 and the names of Thoth.

Further information regarding the numbers 52 and 65 is also very interesting. There are different series of numbers. You can count from 1 through 10 by simply going 1, 2, 3, 4, 5, 6, 7, 8, 9,etc. but you could also double such as with the digital series: 1, 2, 4, 8, 16, 32, 64, etc. In nature the so-called Fibonacci series is used. For example how the leaves on a plant duplicate; 1, 1, 2, 3, 5, 8, 13, 21, 34, etc. But: something strange is going on here; the numbers 52 and 65 constantly stand out.

Series	Fibonacci numbers	Alpha value	Accumulated Alpha
1	1	1	1
2	1	1	2
3	2	2	4
4	3	3=1+1+2+3=> 7	
5	5	5	12

Crop Circles, Gods and their Secrets

6	8	8	20
7	13=1+3=4>	4	24
8	21	3	27
9	34	7	34
10	55	1	35
11	89	8	43
12	144	9	52
			(52=4x13=52)
13	233	8	8
14	377	8	16
15	610	7	23
16	987	6	29
17	1597	4	33
18	2584	1	34
19	4181	5	39
20	6756	6	45
21	10946	2	47
22	17711	8	55
23	28657	1	56
24	46368	9	65
			(65=5x13=65)
25	75025	1	1
26	212393	1	2
27	196418	2	4
etc....			52
etc....			65
etc....			52

Numerically speaking this is also interesting because in 1998 in England there were several crop circles found with a seven-sided geometrical shape in them. When I asked Bert Janssen, who occupies himself with the geometry of crop circle formations, what the next step would be he said, '"if I'm correct the next step would be an 11 sided geometrical shape". When I look at the numbers 52 and 65 with numerical logic I come to this conclusion; 52 = 5+2=7, and 65= 6+5=11. Coincidence?

52, the game of Thoth

In the script near Alton-Barnes in 1991 we were able to see the names of Ea, Enki, and Ptah. We were also introduced to a bit of Egyptian history. The gods also left their tracks there, just like in other parts of the world. Thoth was one of the gods from the Anunnaki but was a descendent from a much higher dimension than the other gods who came from the fourth dimension. In my opinion Thoth was incarnated to set right what the Anunnaki had ruined considering the Anunnaki came from a lower dimension than Thoth. In my opinion the 'game of Thoth of 52' is one of the things he wanted to accomplish so that we would not have to continue to be abandoned in a two-strand DNA but could advance into a twelve-strand DNA.

During my quest for answers I thought more and more about the possibility of there being Uranium underneath the Great Pyramid which is responsible for keeping mankind imprisoned in a twostrand DNA. On an act of impulse I went to have a look at which atomic number Uranium has. It has the number 92. At number 52 on the table that I was looking at, showed me that Tellurium has the number 52. Somehow I suspected that Uranium and Tellurium are elements that have very similar properties. Further along on my quest for Tellurium and the accompanying number 52 I came across a few very striking matters.

One of those things was that if I add 52 and 92, the result is 144, a Gematrian Number (see section on Gematrian numbers).Another things was the Kramer's version of the Dutch Dictionary depicting the word Tellurium as an apparatus by which the movements of the Earth and the Moon and the movements of the Earth around the Sun are conducted/introduced. It goes on to say that it is also; a chemical element that appears in small quantities in various ores: Its properties correspond to Sulphur.

Stonehenge has been built to keep an eye on the movement of the Earth, the Moon, and the Sun, therefore it could be described as a Tellurium. In his book 'The First Age' Sitchin tells us how detailed

Stonehenge has been formulated. Alford tells us that Stonehenge just as well as Machu Pichu are the works of… Thoth! The angle of the Great Pyramid in Egypt is …52 degrees. We also have 52 weeks in a year. As we have read previously the number 52 was not an unknown number to the Mayan's as a matter of fact the opposite is true. Acting on an inspiration I further went to check out our country's map and to my big surprise discovered that in the Netherlands, I live around the 52 degrees latitudinal line. The area in the south of England where the most beautiful crop circle formations have been found for years lies between the 51 and 52 degrees Latitudinal line. Numerically speaking 52 is a 7 (5 + 2 = 7), and the 7 is a holy number of old, which as I had concluded earlier comes from the Anunnaki who designated the Earth as the 7th planet. On Sumerian clay tablets the Earth is represented by 7 dots.

It is very interesting to note that at the time of the submerging of Atlantis the people of Atlantis made several 'time capsules' made of indestructible metal in which they put their 'Ageless Wisdom, history and knowledge'. The material was the same metal that their flying saucers were made of, and that material was called…'Tellurium'.

Tellurium

Finding these references to Tellurium to be very intriguing I continued my search to discover if it was possible that there could be more information hidden in this concept than what was first visible. I was able to find out the following about Tellurium; the German scientist Franz Joseph Muller Von Reichenstein first discovered Tellurium in 1782; it was recognised as an element and given its name in 1798 by the German chemist Martin Heinrich Klaproth. Tellurium ranks about 78th in natural abundance among the elements in the Earth's crust. In 1000 tons of the Earth's crust there are approximately 2 grammes of Tellurium present and is found during the mining of gold, silver, copper, lead and nickel. Tellurium deposits are found in Mexico, South America, Western Australia, and Ontario, Canada. In the United States, small amounts of the element are obtained from rocks in Colorado and California. Colloidal tellurium is an insecticide, germicide, and fungicide.

Tellurium is a somewhat brittle material, and pulverises easily. It can be used in combination with other metals as a semiconductor. It is also added to copper and steel in scant proportions to improve the tension. If it is added to lead it improves the strength and the resistance against corrosion. The biological concentration in the environment is generally very low and does not create any damage. When there is a high exposure, such as in a metallurgical company it's distinguishing features are a garlic odour, which comes out through your breath, urine and sweat. When the exposure is too concentrated there is permanent damage to the liver, kidneys, heart and central nervous system.

A very interesting fact is that when Tellurium is added to lead, the lead becomes stronger. When I had previously asked the question as to what Tellurium could be added to I received lead as an answer. Consequently it could be possible that the gods of Nibiru (who were inhabitants or co-inhabitants of Atlantis) mixed Tellurium with lead. The Tellurium canisters that Thoth concealed were made of an indestructible metal that no other metal or any bacterium was a match for. When Uranium decays and is no longer radioactive it is called…lead. Imagine that Thoth mixed Tellurium with Uranium so then it doesn't surprise me at all that even the strongest moulds and bacteria could not survive let alone manipulate their way into the capsules and that is why the 'Ageless Wisdom' of Atlantis remains untarnished right up until today. I do believe the same idea applies to the strength of this metal that when it is mixed in the right combination then the end result is a powerful, indestructible metal.

One of the reasons the Anunnaki came to Earth was to mine gold. Is it strange to presume that together with all the gold and other elements that they brought up that the Anunnaki also knew of Tellurium and the applications of it? It is questionable if the Anunnaki were really even looking for gold or did they need Tellurium for their spaceships? The Mayan's had many gold things. If the gods were really crying out for gold then why did the Mayans have gold in abundance? Were the inhabitants of Nibiru looking for something else here instead of the gold as was originally thought?

Earlier on I told you about Thoth (in Atlantis Thoth's name was Chiquitet Arlich Vomalitis) who as a sort of Moses went in a type of spaceship to Egypt, Peru and Tibet to hide the 'Emerald Tablets' after the submersion of the last part of Atlantis. An interesting fact is that during the submersion of Atlantis the inhabitants made several time capsules in which they placed their ageless wisdom, history and knowledge. These capsules were made of the same material as their flying saucers and it was called Tellurium. Could it have been Thoth who was responsible for hiding these capsules? Is it a coincidence that a Tellurium is an apparatus by which the movement of the Earth and the Moon and the movement of the Earth are demonstrated just as Stonehenge and Machu Pichu which are also the works of Thoth.

The crop circle code

You could say that for at least the last 25 years mankind has been 'treated' to thousands of mysterious crop circles. These formations vary from simple, uncomplicated circles in the early years to very complex geometric formations at the end of the nineties. Professor Gerald Hawkins has found the 'diatonic ratios' in this last category of formations. These 'diatonic ratios' can be converted into letters out of which the names of different people appear. All these people had one thing in common; they were the first 25 presidents of the 'Society for Physical Research of London'. Hawkins also translated the 1991 inscription of Milk Hill. He translated it as 'Opono Astos'. Michael Green translated this inscription as Ea, Enki and Ptah, which are one and the same. We have also been able to read what kind of history lays behind this Ea, Enki, and Ptah. It is a history that can solve many of the mysteries of the past as long as man (one) is prepared to let go of their deep-rooted ideas and look at the past with a broad new outlook.

We have also been able to read the messages that were hidden in the crop circles. At a first glimpse the messages are not legible and one can do nothing with them. The coincidence was that with the deciphering of the inscription a mirror was brought into the picture in which it was discovered that the mirrored inscription contained a Hebrew sentence which said; 'sewet chm anasim gadasim', or rather 'a new breed of people'. A somewhat surprising result considering the fact that two other persons, by the name of Hawkins and Green who had occupied themselves with the translation, had come up with the same thing. Nevertheless I continued on with this sentence and set up a system from which I thought I had a way to decipher the crop circles.

Ever since I became occupied with the crop circle phenomenon I have always asked myself in which way the creators code the eventual messages in the crop circles. Naturally you could think of all kinds of complicated constructions but in my opinion it should be a code that is quite simple. As a matter of fact so simple that it can easily be overlooked. Then I asked myself 'but what is a simple code'? I have discovered that through my decoding system it is really quite simple. Everyone who can count to ten and has a grasp of the Hebrew language is capable of cracking this code. I am not saying that I believe that all the crop circles can be deciphered in this manner but just a small section of the thousands of formations that have appeared so far. In my opinion there is a combination of different decoding systems necessary to be able to decipher all the crop circles.

The code cracked

So what exactly does my 'crop circle code' entail? As I mentioned earlier it is a combination between the counting of the circles and the subsequent arising numbers and then to transpose them into Hebrew. It sounds easier than it is and that is why with the use of an example I will show you a few possibilities to clarify what comes to pass when you are in the process of deciphering a crop formation. Even when all the number combinations have been translated into a word or a sentence there exists the possibility that, just as was the case with the inscription, there could be a 'false bottom' or ' hidden message' in it. So as you can see there is a lot of puzzling involved before a complete formation has been deciphered. For the example I have chosen the DNA formation of 1996 particularly as I had the exact information to hand (see photograph).

When I started occupying myself with the worldwide occurring crop circle formations it didn't take me very long to discover that the least you had to be capable of was counting to ten. The next part would be that you should have mastered the Hebrew language. As of yet I truly have not mastered the Hebrew language but I have the good fortune of having a good friend whom comes from Israel. She has been able to help me a great deal with the translating of the Hebrew to Dutch. Other than that a good Hebrew dictionary offers great results.

The Hebrew letters all represent a number value. It starts with the first letter Alep that represents the number 1. Bet, the second letter represents the number 2 and so we can continue on until the letter Tav, which has a number value of 400. Below you will find a summary of the Hebrew language and their number value.

Alep	1	Tét	9	Pé	80
Bét	2	Jot	10	Tsadé	90
Giemel	3	Kaf	20	Kóf	100
Dalét	4	Laméd	30	Résh	200
Hé	5	Mém	40	Shien	300
Vauw	6	Noen	50	Tav	400
Zajin	7	Samék	60		
Chét	8	Ajin	70		

Furthermore there are a number of letters (5) that are added to the Hebrew language that are solely for the purpose of the pronunciation. We are of course referring to the European rendering of the Hebrew script.

The DNA formation consisted of a total of 89 circles. If I examine the number 89 then I can divide it into an 8 and a 9. If I compare the Hebrew alphabet to it then I can see that the numerical value of the letter Chét is an 8. In turn I do the same with the number 9. The Hebrew letter Tét has the numerical value of 9. The combination of both letters gives us a translation of 'not officially' which is exactly right because the DNA formation officially consists of 90 circles, this we know because there was one hidden circle. This hidden counter clockwise turning circle was found underneath one of the clockwise circles. The number 90 means 'flying', and isn't that what the gods from long ago did?

In this manner it is possible to translate all the numbers in certain crop circle formations. The numbers from a formation can be seen as individual numbers or can also be seen as tenths or hundredths. For example the number 89 is built out of 80 + 9, only this number (80 + 9) is not translatable, but the mirrored image number 90 + 8 does. The translation of this number is 'clear'. This is how the same number can be worked out to have several different translations according to how the number is being deciphered either as an addition, a sum or as a reflected number.

Crop Circles, Gods and their Secrets

Furthermore we can take the number 89 and make a few more translations such as 8 x 9 = 72. If we search the Hebrew alphabet for the numbers 7 and 2 we come to the letters Zajin and Bét. This combination means 'flowing'. If we take the mirrored images of 72 we get 27, which means ' despise or disdain'. The number 89 can also be added to get 17, which in turn means 'then, past'. 71 is the reflected number which means 'that is i.e.'.

If we examine the DNA formation more closely then we can see that the formation is constructed out of twelve so called 'chakras'. According to my system of decoding 12 means 'the month of July, August' at the same time 12 means 'father' or 'shoot/sprout'. In my opinion it depends on the rest of the translations of the rest of the different numbers which word should be used from the number 12. 'The month July, August' is a translation that does sort of jump out at you considering there is a graph to see on the website of ' The Noise Room' (www.thenoiseroom.com) where someone has been collecting data from the last 6 years. The graph indicates that in the last few weeks in July and the first week of August is when the most crop circles are formed in England.

The two strands that connect ten of the 12 'chakras' together respectively have 38 and 39 circles however even without adding the ten 'chakras'. The number 38 of the 1st DNA strand cannot be translated but if we split up the number into 30+8 then we get 'vital force = (DNA)'. The mirrored image of this figure gives us 83, which means 'draw a circle, or trace a circle'. The result of 24 when we multiply 3 x 8 gives us 'matter' as a translation while 42 gives a somewhat odd (in my eyes) translation of 'bear'. The combination of 80+3 gives us 2 translations. The first one being 'premature birth' and the second one is 'fade out/away, disappear, become invalid/expire'. The addition of 3 + 8 = 11 does not have a meaning.

The second DNA strand consists of 39 circles, the numbers 3 and 9 gives us 'separation or separation/divorce document' as a translation. Other combinations of these two numbers do not give us any translating possibilities, except for 3 + 9 = 12 which once again gives us 'the month of July/August'.

If we examine the two DNA strands in combination with the ten-chakra points at fiveper strand then we come up with 43 circles for the first strand and 44 for the second strand. The translation of 43 means 'with' while the translation of 44 is 'blood'. The only combination that can possibly be derived from the number 43 is 4 x 3 = 12. The number 44 can be split into 40 + 4, which once again means, 'size'. If we convert the numbers of the two strands then we get 4 + 3 = 7 and 4 + 4 = 8. The only combination that I could make out of these two numbers isn't 87 but the combination of 80 + 7, which gives us 'gold' as a result. The number 8 by itself cannot be translated considering there are too many Hebrew letters that can be combined with this number, but it is a different story with the number 7. The only combination possibility is with the letter Laméd and the letter Résh. The translation of 7 with Laméd (30) is 'passes away/dead' and with the letter Résh (200) it is 'foreigner/alien'.

The history of mankind, written in the grain

In summary you could say that the complete history of mankind is described in the English grain fields. Below follows a short but complete translation as it was found in the DNA formation.

The total amount of circles was 89 and 89 stands for 'not officially' or 'something is not right'. Indeed there was something that was not right about this formation since there were 90 circles. The one strand of circles consisted of 44 circles while the other one consisted of 43 circles. The numbers 43 and 44 mean 'with' and 'blood'. You can calculate the 89 as 8 + 9 = 17, and the meaning of that is 'then or past'. The earlier mentioned number 90 means 'flying' while numerically speaking the result of 43, 44, 89, and 90 are 7, 8, 8, 9, which means 'prediction/prophecy'. A further calculation of the DNA numbers points out that the number 43

(4+3=7) as the 7 only to be read in combination with 200 or 30 gives the following translation; 7/200 = 'stranger/alien' and 7/30 = 'passed away or dead'. Thus far you can say that it says the following' In the past there has been ....with the blood of a passed away or dead alien/foreigner/stranger'. The missing blank of the message could be; .. genetic manipulation' especially considering that the form of the crop circle is an exact reproduction of the human DNA.

The remaining words from the DNA formation are; 'flowing/smooth, clear, separation, vital force (DNA) trace a circle/describe a circle, premature birth/fade away/disappear, invalid/expire, gold bear'. At first glance it seems to be a strange jumble of words, but if we look at these words more carefully then there really is only one word present that I cannot put in it's place. That being the word 'bear'. For the rest I believe that all the words are in connection or related to the gods of the Twelfth planet.

The words 'separation, vital force (DNA) and premature birth all refer to the genetic procedure that the Anunnaki performed on primitive mankind in the distant past. There was a genetic separation/division made between Homo Erectus and 'the new breed of people', the Homo Sapiens. In the eyes of the theory of evolution this is considered to be a premature birth because the theory of evolution tells us that it can take millions of years before an ape evolved into a man. The sudden transition of Homo Erectus to Homo Sapiens still baffles the minds of current day scientists. One simply cannot justify the great enormous transition between the two species. One gets cornered at all anglestrying to explain to the general public how this could be possible. In my opinion, Sitchin is the only one who was able to give a satisfactory explanation for the sudden changeover based on the literal translation of the Sumerian clay tablets. These translations are being contradicted by current day Assyriologists based on the fact that according to them, Sitchin recorded various translational errors in his work. My question is, is this true or have the lady and gentlemen assyriologists taken this completely amiss? According to my opinion I seriously believe so.

When one started with the translations of the clay tablets one came across words such as the Sumerian word DIN.GIR. In a sentence structure situation this word represented a deity/celestial being such as EN.KI. On the clay tablets this is what was written 'DIN.GIR.EN.KI'. According to Assyriologists this means ' the god ENKI'. Supposing DIN.GIR means rocket, which is what Sitchin claims, then it totally loses the Assyriologists because (according to them) in their opinion the word rocket simply has no place on a clay tablet from thousands of years ago. 'In that time civilisation had just started, and they did not know about rockets, and that's a fact (no argument possible)'. So if from the beginning you insist that the translation simply says that DIN.GIR means god and nothing else then, again according to them, Sitchin is indeed wrong with his translation. But what if the assyriologists are wrong and Sitchin isn't? What then?

According to the DNA formation translations and according to Sitchin's translation of the Sumerian clay tablets the separation of the life force (vital force); the DNA was what caused the premature birth of the Homo Sapiens. The words 'flowing and clear' are being used in reference to the planet itself. The Twelfth planet is supposedly a water rich planet, which shines very brightly/clear when the Sun passes it because the Sunlight reflects on the atmosphere and the very tight cloud cover. Flowing refers to the water that is available in overabundance on Nibiru – the planet of the gods. The words 'trace a circle/describe a circle', refer to the orbit of the planet around our Sun. In my opinion these words can also be associated with the making of the crop circle formation, only I'm not quite sure how, but this feeling is purely based on intuition. 'Fade away/disappear', has to do with the fading away and disappearance of this planet after it has passed our Sun. The words 'invalid/expire' can once again be brought into association with the DNA that is becoming invalid to the point of expiration as that is what is currently happening.

During a recent interview with a Dutch magazine, Drunvalo Melchizedek told them that human DNA is indeed changing. According to him there are now children being born with a

Crop Circles, Gods and their Secrets

supernatural DNA. A DNA, which is no longer susceptible to AIDS. Could this possibly be the meaning of the crop circle formation found on the 26th of June 1999 on Arlington Down, that there are now children being born with a three strand DNA? Or is the DNA of mankind changing to prepare us for the transition to another dimension?

The only word I can't place is the word 'bear'. It could be referring to the constellation 'big bear'. Should we be searching in that direction to behold the arrival of the Twelfth planet? According to the Sumerian clay tablets we can expect the arrival of Nibiru to be in the Southern Hemisphere, the only problem being that 13,000 years ago the Earth did a 180° revolution and Nibiru will now be arriving out of the North according to our point of view. When I looked in one of Sitchin's books I saw that the Bible book of Job says that:

> 'Alone he stretches out the heavens,
> and treads upon the farthest Deep.
> He arrives at the Great bear, Orion and Sirius,
> And the constellations of the south'.

'Gold' is the word that remains. Sitchin tells us that the Anunnaki came to the Earth to dig up gold for their planet. Apparently the gold was brought into Nibiru's atmosphere as gold dust because the Anunnaki had spoiled Nibiru's atmosphere to such an extent that it was no longer able to resist negative influences.

My intuition told me that there was more information concealed in the formation than that. Information that was of importance and that I should be able to bring to the surface because I had already discovered long ago that there are double meanings present in every translation. Just when I thought I had discovered everything then something highly unlikely surfaced which in turn reinforced the translations.

Following you will see a different approach, which indicates that the exact data (specifications) of a formation is very important with regard to the deciphering of that formation. What else could there be to calculate? I really thought I had calculated it all but looking back it wasn't so. After calculating and re-examining the DNA formation several times I had a look as to what I could do with the specifics of the length of the DNA formation. The full length of the DNA formation is 197.5 metres long and in my opinion there was more information concealed in the dimension of this formation. The only question being now is how do we calculate this length and what do we do with it?

I asked myself as to how I should further calculate this formation. I felt as though I could not calculate this in metres considering there are many more units of measurement then just metres. It made me think of the Egyptian unit of measurement that is very similar to the modern day English inch. In the Great Pyramid you come across a unit of measurement that is identical to the English inch namely 2.54 centimetres. From this you can conclude that the English standard unit of measurement belongs to the oldest in the world. Later on it will be obvious to you that this comes from the gods. This Great Pyramid which was built 16000 years ago by one of the gods therefore has a unit of measurement contained within which the gods used. From this concept I was able to reason that the length of the DNA spiral should be divided in inches. Next I calculated the length of the DNA formation with the English standard unit of measurement which means that I took the length of 197.5 metres and divided it by an inch, a foot, and a yard. The following is the results:

197.5: 0.0254 = 7775,590551   rounded off; 7776

197.5: 0.0348 = 647,9658792651   rounded off;   648

197.5: 0.9144 = 2115,9886264   rounded off;   216

Some time later I placed a Hebrew letter underneath each letter and spent a very long Tuesday morning battling figures and trying to solve the quotient but these numbers would not let themselves be translated in the same manner as I was able to do with the other numbers. This was a bit strange more so because when I counted the circles of the DNA spiral on an individual basis it did work and now I had to figure out a different method to approach this. But how?

More 'DNA numbers'

What other 'evidence' is available? Let's have a look at what kind of results the following numbers give us. We have seen that the length of the DNA formation is exactly 197.5 metres and that is the exact length the formation needed to get to the calculations that I had made earlier. If the formation had been merely 5 centimetres shorter or longer then my calculations would have never come to the numbers that I calculated, precisely 7776, 648 and 216. These numbers are all Gematrian Numbers, as you will see later on.

If I convert these numbers then I get: 7776 = 27 = 9, 648 = 18 = 9 and 216 = 9. As an end result I then have 27, 18 and 9. If I place these numbers in a row with the 9 in front, then I get 9 1 8 2 7. These numbers have the following meaning;

$$918 = \text{doing something that's not allowed}$$
$$18 = \text{struck on the material}$$
$$82 = \text{guilty}$$
$$27 = \text{despise}$$

If I compare these results to the earlier discovered message from the DNA formation, which says that 'in the past one has genetically interfered with the blood of a survivor/dead stranger', then the above-mentioned discovery is pretty odd. Indeed the gods were guilty of something. They genetically interfered with the course of mankind. They did something that isn't allowed and set us back with a two-strand DNA of the original twelve-strand DNA. The gods permanently placed us (locked us into) a two-strand DNA which in other words says that we only deal from our bottom two chakra's. These are the basic and the abdominal chakra's. The first one connects the individual with the physical world surrounding him or her and the second one is the centre of your sexual energy. If you look around carefully, then you can see that the majority of the population does indeed keep themselves occupied with these two things, precisely sex and materialism. Few have yet come in touch with their spiritual being but there is hope.

The result of 'struck on materialism doesn't surprise me considering we really are connected to the material world. In summary you could say that the complete message says; 'because the gods did something that wasn't allowed (from higher up), one despised mankind and was guilty because the gods condemned mankind into the materialistic aspect of things forever'.

Gematrian numbers

After a few days off with a well-deserved break a very interesting article caught my eye that talked about the 'THE CODE of Carl Munck and Ancient Gematrian Numbers'. In this article the author amongst other things tells us that these 'Gematrian numbers' are most likely thousands of years old. In my opinion these numbers go back to the time of Atlantis, considering the Great Pyramid plays a large role in the calculating of these numbers. Further on I will demonstrate and prove to you that the Great Pyramid is actually older than has been presumed up until now which proves that the numbers of the 'Code Gang' are very old. For those of you who are interested in these numbers, I would like to refer you to the web site of the 'Code Gang' which is; http://www.greatdreams.com/gem1.htm 'The Code Gang' is what Joe Mason, Michael Morton, James Furia, Craig Tuz, Dee Finney and Gary Val Tenuta call themselves. This 'gang' took the Carl Munck's discovered code and did various recalculations as far as some very old and holy places and constructions such as Stonehenge, Rennes-le-Chateau and Bethlehem were concerned. They discovered that the prime meridian as we know it did not run across Greenwich in earlier times but exactly across the Great Pyramid of Giza. They calculated the difference between Greenwich and Giza and in this manner they were able to calculate the number s of the old 'grid' of the Earth. What it literally comes down to is that a construction such as Stonehenge no longer lies at 1 degree 49 mins and 29 sec but according to Gematrian numbers it lies at 21,600 North. The 'Code Gang' has decoded many old monuments in this manner. The numbers from Stonehenge can also be written as 216 without the zeroes. The number 216 bring us back to Plato who many centuries earlier wrote and I quote ' What is of divine origin has a circumference, which is contained in a perfect number'. Scholars have calculated that this number is indeed 216.

The 'strange' thing about all these numbers is that they are all-dividable and can be multiplied by the number nine. The Tangent of 36, 216, 1296 and 3456 is + 0.726542528. The numbers 144, 864, 2304 and 5184 create the same Tangent, only the plus (+) needs to be replaced by a minus (-). We see the same when we see the numbers 72, 52, 432, 1152 and 2592. The tangent of this is +3.077683537, while 108, 288, 648, 1728 and 3888 have a negative Tangent (a – instead of a +). The Numerical sum of all these numbers is nine, example; 2 + 5 + 9 + 2 = 18 = 9.

The article of the 'Code Gang' also mentions that 6 raised to the third power (6 x 6 x 6), gives us 216. I reasoned with my self that if this was so then what was the answer to 6 to the power of 4 or to the power of 5? The first 6 x 6 x 6 x 6 gave an answer of 1296, while the sum of 6 to the power of 5 gave 7776 as a result. At first instance it doesn't seem to be a significant answer but the number 7776 stood out because it was the rounded off figure of the length of the DNA formation when divided by inches! The other calculations were rounded off to 216 and 648. Without knowing it I had discovered ancient Gematrian Numbers in a grain circle in this manner. The only thing was that 648 didn't really fit into the realm of the same Tangent calculations because 648 had a different Tangent than 216 and 7776. What is striking is that the numbers 219, 648, and 7776 all have 1 x 9, 2 x 9, and 3 x 9, therefore, 9, 18, 27 as a result.

What is also amusing is the fact that when you multiply the 12 'chakras' (successive focal points) of the DNA formation with 648 then you get 7776. In ancient times the ancient Babylonians used a method of measurement to determine volume and this was known as 'Maneh'. At present the volume of 21,600 'Um', is measured as 7776 cubic inches, which is 197.5 cubic centimetres, which again is the length of the DNA spiral in metres.

After taking the same calculations and applying them to the sizes of the inscription at Milk Hill I discovered that in the highest point of the script, namely 5.5 metres, the almost exact same numbers popped up like 6, 18, and 216! What is even more fun is that if you take 18 and multiply it by 216, then the result is 3888 and 3888 is half of 7776. Is it a coincidence that after calculations are complete the same Gematrian Numbers appears in two totally separate crop circle formations? I don't think so.

What is also an interesting factor is that in the article it says that the number 2160 is also the exact diameter measurement in miles of our Moon. Thus Plato's number 216 x 10. Plato had another number (See Plato, the State VIII, 545-546) which is 1296 and that number can be found in the inscription, namely as 18 x 216 = 1296. Then to continue 1296 is contained in half the precessional figure that the Sumerians had calculated thousands of years ago. According to them the precession of the equinoxes around the ecliptic was a process that took 25,920 years (2592 and 1296 are Gematrian numbers). The Egyptians had calculated the precession cycle as 12 x 2150 = 25,800. This last number has a 6 as a Numerical calculation (2 + 5 + 8 + 0 + 0 = 6) while you look at the current day figures and calculations this appears to be a nine, namely 25,776 = 27 = 9.

Since we are currently on the topic of the number nine I would like to bring you back to the subject of Tellurium. Is it a coincidence that the melting point of Tellurium is 450 degrees and the boiling point is reached at 990 degrees? Both numbers can be converted into... 9.

The speed of light in millennia old numbers

What did the ancient peoples know more than what we know today and from who did they receive the knowledge about the 'Gematrian Numbers'? And who was it that was capable of calculating these numbers thousands of years ago? Which people had a 'supercomputer' that was able to calculate all these statistics? Who was able to take the two Tangent calculations of 3.077683537 and 0.726542528 multiply them and get 2.236067977 as a result. This number is the square root of five which itself is a Tangent calculation namely the Tangent of 186,234.09485. This last figure is the exact speed of light in the air in miles per second! The speed of light in a vacuum, is, the article continues, 186,234.5894 miles per second. The Tangent of 186,234.09485 = 2.236067197552 − 2.23660067977 = 0.00000779473440429. According to my opinion it is a negligible difference to 7799473440429 billionth of a mile! Who was knowledgeable of such calculations and numbers at that time? Perhaps they were of the same gods that created mankind? What is it that 'they' want to clarify to us now? Why are these certain 'Gematrian Numbers' appearing in the crop circles?

A return of the gods in 2012?

One explanation could be that the number 216 could be seen as 2160, which is one-twelfth of the precession cycle. The same applies to the number 648 if you add the 0. 6480 is 3 x 2160. Add 216, 648, and 7776 together and you get 8640 which is exactly 4 x 2160. The remarkable thing of the number 7776 as 777,600 is that it is exactly 2160 x 360. This last calculation refers to one-twelfth of the precession cycle times 360 days. There are very strong indications that before the great flood the Earth completed its journey around the Sun in 360 days and therefore 1 year had 360 days. After the great flood this changed and the Earth now needs 5 more days to complete the full rotation. As I go further along I am under the assumption that the revolution time of Nibiru the planet of the gods is not 3600 years but 'merely' 2160 years especially considering one writes 2160 as 3600 in Sumerian!

$$\frac{3600 \quad 600 \quad 60 \quad 10 \quad 1}{3 \quad 6 \quad 0 \quad 0} = 2160$$

Does 7776 in the DNA formation mean that the planet of the gods will re-enter our solar system every 777,600 days? In other words, every 2160 years? If we open the magic trick box of Numerology even further we can take the present day precession cycle of 25,776 and convert it. We can do this by taking the 2 and the 5 and adding them up together and this is how we would get to 7,776 as an end result. 7776 is a 'precession number', considering that 3 times 2592 (2592/0), gives 7776 (7776/0) as a result. Are we slowly being prepared for the return of the Nibiru by subtle hints in the various crop circle formations? If this is so, then when can we expect the planet that carries our creators?

In general it is presumed that this planet last passed the Sun in 200 BC. In this calculation it is presumed that the revolutionary time is 3600 years. The next passage of the planet would be around the year 3400. This period has been calculated considering the fact that around 7400 and 3800 BC the civilisation of Sumeria suddenly re-flourished. It is a fact that during a passage of the planet of Nibiru the gods taught mankind various things. I take the view that this assumption is not quite right considering that in my theory there is a longer period of time needed to coerce a complete civilisation to a higher evolution. In my opinion you cannot make an allegation that once the planet has passed ours that civilisation will be lifted to a higher level in one big bang. This needs an introductory or transitional period. This is also considering the fact that in 1958 an archaeological team under the guidance of a prehistoric expert by the name of James Mellaart discovered a very old Neolithic village in Anatolia. The name of this village is Çatal Hüyük, near present day Konya, and it had a whole network of internally connected homes and an extraordinarily advanced civilisation, which was established as early as 8500 to 700 BC. One could never have had the faintest idea that such a civilisation existed in the Middle East. This is also due to the fact never before had evidence been found in that direction. So well before 7400 BC there lived an advanced civilisation in the Middle East. So the point of view that Nibiru has a revolution period of 3600 years no longer makes any sense to me because who then helped the civilisation of Çatal Hüyük 'get off the ground'? If you are to assume that every time the planet of the gods passes the Earth, that civilisation flourishes then the revolution period of 3600 years no longer tallies. To me it seems more accurate that it would be a period of respectively 2160 or 2148 years.

The odd thing is that 3 periods of 3600 years is exactly the same amount as 5 periods of 2160 years, precisely 10,800 years. If I take the other numbers from the Milk Hill script and multiply them with each other then I get 108. 6 x 18 = 108, and once again this is a Gematrian number, just as all the other numbers, which I was able to extract from the two formations. If we calculate back in periods of 2160 years right to the great flood around 11,000 BC then we indeed come to the year 200 BC, to be exact 183 BC. Taking this calculation into consideration the next passage of Nibiru would have been in 1977. As far as I can remember there was never a planet that passed by around that date.

A very interesting calculation is when we start to figure backwards from the end of the Mayan calendar, precisely December of 2012. After 6 periods of 2160 years we come up with 10,948 BC. Allan Alford calculated that the great flood took place in 10,983 BC. In between 10,948 and 10,983 BC there is a time difference of merely 35 years. In my opinion a very insignificant time period if you think about the fact that Alford made a calculation of an event that occurred 11,000 years ago. But this theory was not acceptable to me. According to my idea there should be exact calculations possible to determine all the dates and numbers. Especially considering that the end of the Mayan calendar simply offers the end of a cycle of 26,000 years only to begin again at the beginning of the calendar. Or does the ending of the Mayan calendar indicate the return of the Nibiru? Will we be able to meet our creators in person around December of 2012? What did Plato mean with' What is of godly origin has a revolution contained in a perfect number'? Could he have meant that Nibiru would make a 'revolution' based on a 'perfect number'? Will Nibiru return into our solar system after an absence of nearly 2160 years? Is 2160 the perfect number, considering that the numerical result is 9 and 9 is the perfect number. We shall see.

'Fooling' Marduk

After the destructive great flood Enki took it upon himself to rule over Egypt and the African lands. It was later decided with the followers of Enlil, the brother of Enki, that after the period of governing, during the constellation of Leo, that the next three consecutive periods of 2160 years would belong to the followers of Enlil. Marduk knew that his time of ruling would come when the Sun was in the same region of the celestial sphere as the constellation Aries (ram). When Marduk wanted to claim his time of ruling he was told that it was not yet time and that the constellation of Aries was not yet in this narrow belt known as the zodiac. The disagreement between Marduk and Thoth resulted in a fight but Thoth was able to convince Marduk to wait until his time period actually began. The mistake that Marduk made, as Thoth informed him, was that Marduk started calculating from the time of the great flood, precisely 10,983 BC. Thoth was able to fool Marduk by convincing him that the precession of the equinoxes about the ecliptic actually started a degree and a half later than 10,983 BC. A degree and a half taken from the 25,920 years is exactly 108 years. Marduk was satisfied with this answer basically because he did not have access to the means to be able to check these figures, but he did blame Thoth and accused him of meddling with the time. Ultimately one was able to take away 215 years in total from Marduk and consequently he came to power 215 years later than what had been the initial intention.

What kind of consequences does that have for modern day calculations? I started to calculate to see of there is some correlation between the date of the great flood, the length of time of the precession cycle and the end of the Mayan calendar in 2012. I am working with

Crop Circles, Gods and their Secrets

Alford's meticulously calculated date of the great flood, namely 10,983 BC. If I take the periods of Leo (lion), Cancer (crab), Gemini (twins), and Taurus (bull) and reduce them by 10983 then I get 4 x 2160 – 10,983 = 2343. Minus the degree and a half which gave me a result of; 2343 – 108= 2235. Two more time periods were brought to enlightenment after that and they are Aries (ram) and Pisces (fishes). The time period of Pisces probably started around the year 75 BC and will continue through until the year 2085 AD.

Had the gods calculated the precession of the equinoxes of 25,920 years correctly or did they use rounded off figures? If this is the case does Nibiru really have a revolution time of 2160 years or does this time vary? One possibility is that during the calculation of the precession of the equinoxes cycle the Earth's axle stood at a different position than the present day stance of 23.5 degrees. So must a correction for precession be applied to celestial charts to find the true position of the stars? What was the stance of the Earth directly after the great flood? It only has to differ by one degree and you are faced with a totally different result. In between the cycle calculated by the gods and the present day calculations there is a difference of 144 years.

After completing a calculation with the present day precession cycle statistic of 25,776 years (12 x 2148= 25,776) I came up with the following result; 10,983– (6 x 2148) = 1905). We must not forget to add the degree and a half that Marduk was cheated out of. A degree and a half taken from 25,776 years = 107.4 years. It really doesn't make a difference if the precession cycle really started 108 years later as Thoth was able to convince Marduk,or, if in the meanwhile the 108 years have been ' inserted'. The remarkable thing is that if you take the degree and a half of 107.4 years and add it to the 1905 you get a result of 2012.4 AD! The end of the Mayan calendar!

Is it possible that the circle in the middle of the Delphinograms found between July 30th and August 22 1991 represents the fact that Nibiru is halfway on its journey? Could the circle represent the fact that the planet is in the 'neighbourhood' of Pluto, considering that the circle lies close to the 'fins' that according to Steve Canada represent Pluto's orbit? In other words; the planet of the gods is much closer than originally thought. Could this be the reason why NASA wants to launch a telescope and station it in the neighbourhood of Jupiter? Why does this telescope have to be placed so far away? The reason given to the public is that they want to research the galaxies. The closest galaxy is Alpha Centauri, which is 4.3 light years away. If NASA wants to station this telescope close to Jupiter then you can ask yourself (who are they trying to kid) if they are really speaking truthfully. Those 'few' miles that the telescope will be stationed closer to the galaxy to be observed is basically a negligible amount. Could they possibly want to observe an approaching planet? Is the planet of our creators approaching our solar system from a 'strange angle'?

Crop Circles, Gods and their Secrets

5

The crop circle makers reveal themselves

Twelfth Planet?

The fact that the existence of another planet in our solar system can't just be proven is very clear. Thus far it has not been possible for anyone to be able to determine the position of this planet. There are people who say that Sitchin's story is merely based on astrological mythology and that it is nothing more and nothing less than that. Assyriologists are even able tell you that the clay tablets were translated incorrectly by Sitchin.

Reading the book ' Gods of the new Millennium' in 1998, I sent the author Alan Alford an e-mail with several questions regarding his book. I received an e-mail back in which Alford told me that he had got a little carried away and had wanted to unravel too many facts at the same time. He had made a mistake and had come to the conclusion afterwards that the ancient Sumerians did not see gods come out of the heavens but they had seen fragments of an exploded planet that had landed upon the Earth. These fragments were seen as signs of the gods by the ancient Sumerians. The Sumerians were just somewhat confused and they didn't know what they were talking about. I was very surprised by this e-mail because it just didn't seem logical to me that after ten years of thorough research and having written a 500-page book he would deny everything that he wrote and tell me that he had completely missed the point.

My question is: could this be true? Does a twelfth planet really not exist? Did Sitchin incorrectly translate the clay tablets? Is the scientific world correct in saying that there really is a logical explanation for the fact of the sudden transition from Homo Erectus to Homo Sapiens? Has there never been a genetic intervention by outside forces? Did Sitchin make up a tall tale? Is everyone who is preoccupied with Sitchin's research on the wrong track? Did people such as Erich von Däniken get completely carried away? Is there a logical explanation for everything that can prove the opposite of all these facts? I don't think so. I think that the ancient civilisations of the past knew darn well what they were talking about. I have discovered that all the myths, legends, facts and stories that have come from old times all have a double meaning. I feel that the story of the twelfth planet also has a hidden meaning to it – a story to read between the lines. One is the astrological meaning and the second one being the story that is able to tell us how it once was.

But then what's the scoop with the translation of the inscription and that of the DNA formation? In short hand form these two crop circle formations tell us exactly the same story that Sitchin was able to translate (decipher) from the old clay tablets. Was the inscription made by a bunch of jokers? Did the same jokers turn around five years later and pull another stunt by making the DNA formation? If this was the case then these jokers would have an unreal historical knowledge stored 'upstairs' in the brain department. Knowledge that is actually only being rediscovered the last few years. What is the explanation then for the Gematrian numbers that appeared in both formations? I have been suspicious of these formations for a longer period of time already due to the fact that I believe that the Anunnaki gods were responsible for these formations in a manner in which we are not yet capable of comprehending. And what of the numbers that are thousands of years old that have been able to be traced back to the number 9? These are numbers that are assumed to have stemmed from the Anunnaki, the gods of the twelfth planet. If they were so advanced that they could actually colonise another planet then we can say that their knowledge was much more advanced than ours is now. In my opinion it was the Anunnaki who divided the Earth into latitudinal and longitudinal lines of which the prime meridian ran over the Great Pyramid. Ancient places such as Angkor Vat or Easter Island are all situated at a distance of 72 or 144 degrees from Giza. These numbers can all be found in the precession cycle of the Earth and can be converted into 9. The re-calculations made by the 'Code Gang' of these ancient places also allows us to understand that these places were not just situated by chance. According to modern calculations, Stonehenge is no longer situated at the longitudinal and latitudinal lines that it was but it has been re-calculated at 21,600. Bethlehem has been recalculated at 648. These re-discoveries show us nothing but the simple fact that everything in the Universe has been built according to a Universal order which is based on the perfect number 9. In my opinion the Anunnaki were able to construct everything based on this order. But what kind of evidence is there to prove that everything has been formulated according to a Universal order? Let us have a look at the planets currently known to us in our Solar System.

The nine planets

I continued to calculate with reference to an idea that was passed on to me by Chinese astrology. In the Western world the Sun is the centre of astrology. Every month the Sun is located in a different zodiacal sign. The idea that was passed down to me was based on the fact that in Chinese astrology it is Jupiter, which is situated in each one of the zodiacal signs for one year. The current day orbit of Jupiter around the Sun is 11.8 years. Not exactly 12 years but if we do not use the 365.25 days in a year and instead use the 360 days that the year knew before the great flood then oddly enough the result we get is eerily precise, namely 365.25 x 11.870 (= Jupiter's orbit) divided by 360 (= days before the great flood), is 12.04 years. Therefore Jupiter had an orbit of 12.04 years before the great flood. Jupiter is therefore situated for 1 year in every zodiacal sign and revolves for 12 years throughout the zodiacs.

With reference to this idea I started calculating if this would pertain to other planets, but this did not seem to be the case. Jupiter was the only planet that I could associate with the number 12. Next I added up all the diameters of the nine planets and came up with a total of 400,533 kilometres. The numerical value of 400,533 is 15/6 (see table next page).

Mercury	4,878
Venus	12,104
Earth	12,756
Mars	6,787
Jupiter	142,200
Saturn	119,300
Uranus	50,800
Neptune	49,424
Pluto	2,284

After that I started calculating the total circumferences from which I got a result of 1,258,311.53032 kilometres (=400,533x pi). The numerical value of 1,258,311.533032 = 34 = 7.

When we divide 1,258,311.53032 by 9 (the total number of planets) then we get an average of 139,812.3922578 kilometres per planet. The numerical value of 139,812.3922578 = 60/6. The rounded off figure 139,812 also has a numerical value of 24/6. If we divide 400,533 by one mile (=1.6093) then we get 248,886.4723793 miles. Rounded off this is 248,886 = 36/9. The total diameter of the nine planets divided by nautical miles is 216,153.8046411. Unfortunately when this is rounded off it just doesn't quite make 216,153 (18/9). The nautical numbers 216 and 153 are both Gematrian Numbers. The numbers behind the commas have a total value of 2416. Therefore 18 + 6 = 24/6. As you can see we could keep on going and going and going…

Three, Six, Nine = 1:2:3

During my research I continued to stumble across the same numbers. They are the numbers three, six and nine. The number 12 also belongs to this mini – series but 12 is also associated as 1+2=3. In the Egyptian culture plural was not twice but in triplicate form. ' Everything' was known as nine with the Egyptians. When a pharaoh had conquered nine warriors it didn't simply mean that he had conquered nine warriors even though he had defeated all his enemies. The Gematrian

Numbers of the Code Gang are based on the number 6 (60). A half of a degree of the precession cycle of the Earth is 36°; which is 6 x 6. As we have seen earlier the number 216 is constructed from 6 x 6 x 6 = 216. The numbers of the Code Gang presume that the number 6 (or 60) is derived from the Anunnaki because the boss on Nibiru whose name was Anu had the highest order of rank, which was 60.

In my opinion the numbers 3 and 9 also belong to the 6 because everywhere I look I come across the numbers 3, 6 & 9. These numbers form a triad. A triad that represents 1:2:3. Where else do we find these numbers again? If we presume that the Anunnaki were responsible for the Gematrian Numbers then this theory of numbers has to be based on something. Perhaps these numbers are based on a Universal order that is connected to the overall Universal harmony and that it has been built up accordingly based on these numbers. Numbers that each have a specific vibration. If this is true then it should be possible to find more of these kinds of numbers. As far as these types of numbers are concerned let is take a look at which numbers the Earth is concealing.

The diameter of the Earth in km is;	12,756	-21/3
The circumference of the Earth in km is;	40,074	-15/6
The polar circumference of the Earth in km is;	40,024.8	-18/9

Please note that the circumference of the Earth is a rounded off number. The complete number is 40,074.15588919 = 61 = 7! If we take the diameter of the Earth which is 12,756 km and proceed to divide it by a land and a nautical mile and then multiply it by pi, then we respectively get a circumference of land and nautical miles of ; 12,756:1.853 (= nautical miles) = 6883.971937399 x PI = 21626.6356605 = 54/9 and once again the result of these is 12, 9+3=12/3. Is it a coincidence that the result of any number taken at random multiplied by 3, 6 or 9 once converted always has an answer of 3, 6 or 9.?

Since we are on the topic of the numbers 3, 6, and 9 I just want to refer back to the e-mail I received from the I.C.C.A. It was about the discoveries of the 'Milk Hill script' by Gerald Hawkins. The funny thing about this is that Hawkins researched this inscription with a team of 12 (=3) language specialists. He had the choice of 18,000 (=9) variations of 42 (=6) languages. "Coincidentally' we also see the representation of the numbers 3, 6, and 9. Another coincidence?

Proof of a twelfth planet?

Proof of the existence of a planet within our solar system can be found 50 kilometres east of Mexico at a place called Teotihuacán. No one knows who the builders of this city were let alone know the exact names of the various buildings located there. In general it is presumed that Teotihuacán can be dated back to 200 BC. At this time it already took up a surface area of almost 12 square kilometres. From this we can presume that Teotihuacán is from a much older time. Teotihuacán was known to the Aztecs as the ' Place where one could go to sleep and be reborn as a God'. Legends of the Aztecs tell us that it is there in the highlands of Mexico that the Sun and the Moon were born and that it is also where time began. These legends can be found in the two main pyramids of the Teotihuacán, namely the Pyramid of the Sun – one of the largest structures ever built by Native Americans and the Pyramid of the Moon.

One of the strange facts harboured in Teotihuacán is the fact that the Pyramid complex of Teotihuacán conveys our solar system. Along the 'Camino de Los Muertos', the 'Avenue of the Dead' – a broad thoroughfare flanked by ruins of temples which is the main axis of Teotihuacán, lie several buildings. According to the calculations of Hugh Harleston jr. These buildings are harbouring the nine planets of our solar system. Harleston calculated that the builders of Teotihuacán used the smallest measurement that he named the 'Hunab'. This measurement is equal to 1.05954 metres. By using this standard of measurement Harleston was able to calculate that the Earth is situated at a distance of 96 Hunab from the Pyramid of the Sun. Following you will read a summary of the distances of the nine Pyramids/Planets with regard to the Pyramid of the Sun.

Mercury	36 Hunab
Venus	72 Hunab
Earth	96 Hunab
Mars	144 Hunab
Asteroid belt	288 Hunab
Jupiter	520 Hunab
Saturn	945 Hunab
Uranus	1845 Hunab
Neptune	2880 Hunab
Pluto	3780 Hunab

The ' odd' thing about these measurements is that if you multiply these Hunabs with the smallest measurements that Harleston found (1.05954 metres) these measurements can then all be converted to… nine! The Pyramid of Quetzalcoatl lies before the Pyramid of the Sun. Wesley H. Bateman who covers this in full details on his website (www.geocities.com/CapeCanaveral/Hall/3324/tetihuacan.html) tells us that the correct distance between both Pyramids should be 1125 Hunab. It sounds very logical because a distance of 1124 Hunab cannot be converted to 9 in contrast to the rest of the numbers which are almost all able to be converted to 9 except for the 96 Hunab of the Earth and the 520 Hunab of Jupiter. Bateman felt that Harleston had overlooked 1 Hunab.

Hunab = AU

The answer to the question as to why the Earth and Jupiter deviate from the rest of the measurements with regard to the whole complex of Teotihuacán is the following. When I 'accidentally' compared the list of the Hunab distances to the list of Astronomical distances I saw that the AU (Astronomical Unit) of Jupiter was 5.2. The distance from Jupiter in the Teotihuacán complex was 520 Hunab. Suddenly I saw the relationship between both lists. With the distances in Hunab you have to place the decimal 2 places over, which gives the following results (see table next page).

Distance in Hunab with a comma			Distance in AU	
Mercury	0.36	Hunab	Mercury	0.39
Venus	0.72	Hunab	Venus	0.72
Earth	0.96	Hunab	Earth	1.00
Mars	1.44	Hunab	Mars	1.52
Jupiter	5.20	Hunab	Jupiter	5.20
Saturn	9.45	Hunab	Saturn	9.50
Uranus	18.45	Hunab	Uranus	19.20
Neptune	28.80	Hunab	Neptune	30.10
Pluto	37.80	Hunab	Pluto	39.40

What is striking is that if you write the Hunab numbers with the decimal located 2 places over they practically correspond with t he distances that are emphasised in Astronomical distances. Therefore you could suppose that the builders of Teotihuacán used the Hunab as an Astronomical Unit. If I multiply the original distances in Hunab by the smallest measurement of 1.05954 metres discovered by Harleston then the difference between the current Astronomical distance runs anywhere from a mere difference of 0.03 AU for Mercury to a maximal difference of 1.60 AU belonging to Jupiter. When the Hunabs are calculated with the decimal moved two places over the differences become eerily minimal, precisely a minimal of 0.04 AU for Mercury to a maximum difference of 0.55 AU for Pluto (see tables).

	Hunab			AU	Difference
Mercury	0.36 Hunab	Mercury		0.39	0.03
Venus	0.72 Hunab	Venus		0.72	0.00
Earth	0.96 Hunab	Earth		1.00	0.04
Mars	1.44 Hunab	Mars		1.52	0.08
Jupiter	5.20 Hunab	Jupiter		5.20	0.00
Saturn	9.45 Hunab	Saturn		9.50	0.05
Uranus	18.45 Hunab	Uranus		19.20	0.75
Neptune	28.80 Hunab	Neptune		30.10	1.30
Pluto	37.80 Hunab	Pluto		39.40	1.60

Crop Circles, Gods and their Secrets

Hunab					AU	Difference
Mercurius	0,36	x 1,05954 =	0,38	0,39	-0,01
Venus	0,72	,,	0,76	0,72	-0,04
Aarde	0,96	,,	1,01	1,00	-0,01
Mars	1,44	,,	1,52	1,52	0,00
Jupiter	5,20	,,	5,51	5,20	0,31
Saturnus	9,45	,,	10,01	9,50	0,51
Uranus	18,45	,,	19,55	19,20	0,35
Neptunus	28,80	,,	30,51	30,10	0,41
Pluto	37,80	,,	40,05	39,40	0,55

Did one similarly manage the Hunab thousands of years ago as we currently use the Astronomical Unit? Is the Hunab simply an Astronomical Unit? Why are there minimal differences between the Hunabs and the AU's? Do the distances in Hunabs give us a positioning of the planets of thousands of years ago? Possibly the positions of the planets before the great flood? Who built Teotihuacán, or rather, who gave the instructions for the construction? Could it perhaps be the same beings that are responsible for the various crop circle formations? Formations that can tell us of the history of man. What are 'they' trying to make clear to us by means of buildings that are thousands of years old and by present day crop circle formations? Are they trying to warn us or is it that we should be well aware of our past before we can attempt to find out what the future will bring us?

When Tutankhamen's golden tomb was discovered they found a golden strip within it with the following words on it 'I have seen the past, I know the future'.

7200 Hunab = Nibiru

Upon further research Harleston learned that at a distance of 7200 Hunab from the Pyramid of the Sun there was a ruin located there. According to Harleston's calculations this ruin represented Planet X. Planet X, otherwise known as Sitchin's twelfth planet Nibiru is located at 75 AU from the Sun which is equal to 11,250 million kilometres. This distance is ten times the distance of Hunab from the Pyramid of Quetzalcoatl to the Pyramid of the Sun. 1125 Hunab x 10 = 11,250 (million kilometres). Why is the Pyramid of Quetzalcoatl located at exactly 1125 Hunab from the Pyramid of the Sun? Did the builders of Teotihuacán perhaps want to indicate in some small way that there was another complex located at a much further distance from this complex? This was a complex at a distance of 7200 Hunab, which is supposed to represent the planet Nibiru – the planet of the gods. Harleston called this complex the appropriate name of Xiknalkan, which means 'Flying Snake' which brings us back to the gods of Nibiru again.

Coincidence? I don't think that this is a coincidence. The builders of Teotihuacán did not know of coincidences. Everything was built according to a pre-ordained plan - a plan that mankind can still refer to thousands of years later about what once took place a very long time ago. This would be the story of the creation of man by gods of another planet. The same story can be found today in the world-wide crop circle formations.

Is the Delfinogram also a message from the Anunnaki?

Is there proof to be found only in Teotihuacán that there is another member of our Solar System or are there also indications in the English grain fields that point to another planet? At one point I remembered the opinion of the American, Steve Canada. His theory talks of the so-called 'Delfinograms' that appeared in England during the period of July 30 until August 22, 1991. In that period a total of seven appeared. Once again we are confronted with the holy number seven! It is Canada's opinion that the delfinogram reproduces Nibiru's orbit (see illustration).

Crop Circles, Gods and their Secrets

The two outside rings could represent the farthest points of Nibiru's orbit. The ring to the farthest right represents where Nibiru was located at its halfway point (probably around 1800 AD), and the other ring represents the point where the planet will orbit around our Sun. In the middle of the delfinogram there is defined a circle, flattened in the grain, which would represent the current position of Nibiru, in other words halfway through it's orbit which takes a total of 3600 years.

If the 'planet of the gods' truly passed the Earth around 200 BC for the last time then it would mean that the planet would be halfway round it's orbit around our Sun in the year1800 and that it would be on it's return to our solar system. That would mean that the next crossing would be in about 1400 years around the year 3200 AD (I will certainly refer back to all this data especially considering the fact that it is not impossible that the actual date 3200 AD will occur much sooner on the calendar! See also 'Fooling Marduk').

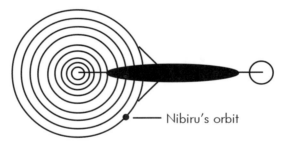

Nibiru's orbit

According to the 'American' the fins of the delfinogram represent the orbit of the nine planets known to us up until now. The outside orbit is Pluto's orbit (see illustration next page). In the Inca temple in Cusco in Peru there is a drawing, which can be seen that shows the reproduction of the orbit of our nine planets together with a very oblong long oval, which could signify Nibiru's orbit. The drawing at Cusco and the delfinogram have a lot of similarities.

Other symbols of the inhabitants of Nibiru have been found in the grain fields besides these significant symbols mentioned previously. One of those is the symbol that belongs to Ninhursag, (also called Ninmah) the Mother Goddess who along with Enki/Ptah created the human race. The horseshoe shaped instrument represents a knife by which the umbilical cord was severed (see illustration below).

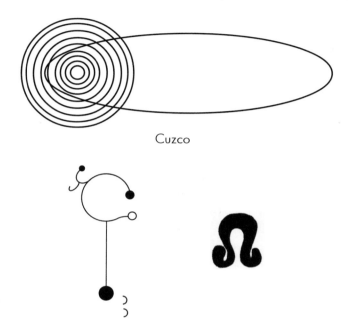

Cuzco

Is it the intention of the gods of Nibiru to make matters clear to us by means of messages in crop circles? If this is the case then how do we recognise that these are the 'messages' of the gods? Are there more crop circles that conceal the symbols of the Anunnaki? Steve Canada has written a lot of books in which he describes the symbols of the gods, and I believe so, because haven't we been able to see what the symbol was for the mother goddess Ninharsag? The other symbols that I have come across are the trident, the symbol of Marduk (see illustration next page).

In this illustration Marduk is killing the monster 'Tiamat' (Earth). The 'horns' that were cited various crop circles represents the identification sign of the Anunnaki. There exists a misunderstanding that the gods had horns on their heads. I think that the horns are only visible in their aura's (see illustrations next page).

Crop Circles, Gods and their Secrets

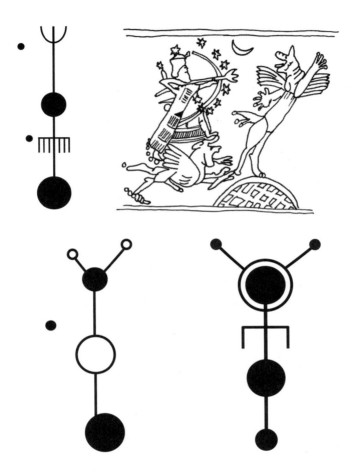

Decoded crop circles

In the last part of this book I want to show the reader a few more examples of messages that are hidden in various formations. Unfortunately I am not able to decipher a formation completely. This is mainly due to the fact that I do not have all the essential information at my disposal. I had contacted various people who keep themselves occupied with the crop circle formation phenomenon to no avail. The only question I proposed was if the person in question could assist me with the exact measurements of a few of the formations. It appeared that no one had the exact dimensions that I was looking for. What was even stranger was that the information I was looking for simply does not exist. Even in the world's largest crop circle information archives managed by Colin Andrews the measurements that I needed were not available.

In this way I want to emphasise to you the utmost importance of the dimensions of a crop circle formation. Even the distances between the circles are important. This distance was something that Joe Mason of the Code Gang used in his calculations. The comprehensive coverage of his findings can be read at (http://www.greatdreams.com/gem7.htm) the website of the Code Gang.

As I went along I got the overall impression that all over the world there are masses of people who keep themselves occupied with the mysterious crop circle formation phenomenon. In all their research efforts and in trying to solve the mysteries one very important thing is forgotten every time and that is: to exactly measure the formations and write down the dimensions. I was completely surprised to discover how few of the formations are actually measured. The more I looked into this the more I got the impression that the people who occupy themselves with the mysterious crop circle phenomenon actually don't really want this phenomenon to be solved. I came to this conclusion after I sent a lot of people an e-mail requesting information on dimensions. The majority of the people just simply did not respond, the odd person made an effort to return an e-mail but was not able to help me. I won't go into further details but it almost drove me up the wall. The most important data that I needed to decipher the crop circles just doesn't seem to be available. More and more I got the feeling that some want to preserve the veil of secrecy that surrounds this phenomenon .

It seems to be to me that we're all working towards the same goal but nobody wants the puzzle to be solved. If we would combine all our forces we would then be capable of reading all the information that is concealed in the various formations. These

Crop Circles, Gods and their Secrets

would be messages that would be useful to mankind. We could learn something from them.

Personally I always ask myself why a formation is the way it is. Why was the length of the DNA formation exactly 197.5 metres? Why did the formation have exactly that many circles within it? Why not one circle more or one circle less? Why not a half a metre longer or a half a metre shorter? Do you know why? Because if a formation contains one or more circles more or less then the original message is no longer translatable or it just becomes incoherent. This is also the same with reference to the length of the found formations. They aren't made 'just like that' without any reason. There is a sound, reliable reason as to why a formation is the way it is.

To me it doesn't seem enough to only measure the crop circles to be able to decipher them. Especially since I have a strong suspicion that there are more 'groups' responsible for the making of the crop circles. If we would be able to find out the code for each group then we would be capable of looking at the crop circle phenomenon in a different light. We would then be able to read the message and understand what they are trying to make clear to us. Up until then it is pure guesswork regarding the rest of the messages that are hidden in the crop circles. These messages are waiting for the moment that there is someone capable of reading these messages on our Earth. By means of the Gerald Hawkins' discovered diatonic ratios and the 'crop circle code' developed by myself or a combination of both we are now able to decipher merely a fraction of the crop circles. The beginning is here, but now we have the rest to do.

Esterick Park Estate, 21 June 1999

The striking thing about the formation that was found on the 21-June-1999 close to Esterick Park Estate is that according to me it harbours the number 80. According to some people you can see two eyes and a mouth when you turn the formation. I find that the 'odd' thing about this crop circle is that there are two circles beside the 8.

Is this an indication that 'something' should be divided by 80? If this is the case then what is it that should be divided by 80?

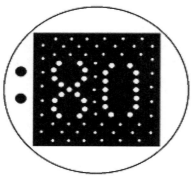

After looking through my data I came to the conclusion that during the crop circle formation season of 1999 there were only two formations that strongly resembled each other. This was the previously mentioned formation and the formation of Windmill Hill, which was found on the 16th of July 1999 (see photograph).

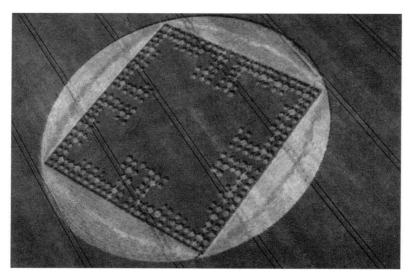

This formation consisted of 288 circles (288 = 4 x 72). The total amounts of circles attracted my attention immediately because of the fact that 288 is a Gematrian Number and can be converted to 9.

The idea that I should divide these two formations by each other would not leave my train of thought because the total number of circles, 110 (31 large and 79 small circles) doesn't really give me a complete translation due to the fact that there are too many numbers (words) missing. This leads me to presume that within the decoding system that I have developed there is still a code, which works purely with numbers (measurements).

I started counting again and much to my amazement I was shown a few remarkable calculations. In my opinion the first calculation seemed to be the most logical, namely 288 divided by 80, which has a result of 3.6. And 3.6 without the decimal is 36 which is also a Gematrian Number. Besides that 36 is also a half a degree of the 25,920 year precession cycle of the Earth. Furthermore I was able to come up with the following calculations from these 2 numbers; $80 \div 288 = 0.277777$, and the two reflected versions, namely $8 \div 882 = 0.0090702$ and $882 \div 8 = 110.25$. I also multiplied the two numbers together; $80 \times 288 = 23040$ and the reflected version $8 \times 882 = 7056$. All these calculations except for $80 \div 288 = 0.277777 = 37 = 1$ can be converted to 9. In my opinion the number that jumps out at me immediately is 23040, because the length of a side of the Great Pyramid of Giza has been scientifically determined as 230.40 meters. If the number is written as 2304 then it is a Gematrian Number.

West Kennet Longbarrow, 4 August 1999

The formation that appeared on the 4th of August 1999 in West Kennet was situated in a remote place in the countryside of Avebury. In this quiet, laid-back, place an observation of a UFO was made which could possibly be connected to this formation. Up until now the shape of this formation has not yet been observed. It seems as if this formation is the 'inside' of a formation that was found on the 16th of July 1999 at Windmill Hill.

The pattern of this formation is truly beautiful because of the three dimensional image that can be clearly seen from above. It seems as if the grain is lying upwards, but it is simply the reflection of the Sun that gives this effect. To make this clear I have made the drawing with two different shades of grey. With the play of light in the field you can see a three dimensional image containing a total of 17 'pyramids' which are enclosed by 120 circles.

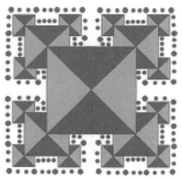

This formation attracted my attention because of the magnificent three-dimensional image. Three dimensional crop circles have been found before but none truly as remarkable as this one.

Considering I do not have access to the complete information to be able to decode the formation completely I do want to take the tip off the iceberg simply by counting the circles.

This formation had a total of 120 circles that I could divide into two groups. One group of 36 large circles and one group of 84 small

Crop Circles, Gods and their Secrets

circles. The number 120 has no meaning but if it is seen as the number 12 then this can be translated into ' the month of July/August'. The mirror image of 12 comes up as 21 and when translated means 'coming'. This number appears fairly regularly in various crop circles and it is a Jewish month, and as we have seen earlier most crop circle formations are formed around the end of July, the beginning of August. We have come across the number 12 before in the DNA formation and I think that the number 12 appears in various formations, this could have to do with the twelfth planet. A planet which the ancient Sumerians tell us without a doubt was part of our solar system and that is how the total amount of planets including the Sun and the Moon make it a complete 12. If we take the amount of 'pyramids' found in this formation and put it under the magnifying glass then we can see that there are 17 in total. The meaning of 17 is 'then or past'.

36, the total number of large circles can be translated as 'there is more to it than meets the eye'. We are all under the assumption that there is more to these mysterious crop circles but the question is what exactly could it be? The number of small circles, 84 to be precise, can be translated as 'giving up a mystery', which makes sense to me because why else would this formation look like it is a three dimensional reproduction of several of the pyramids? Is that the mystery behind this formation? Could it be that part of the solution lies in the Pyramids of Egypt? Is this where we can find out about the advancement of mankind? Previously I have already mentioned that Uranium is buried beneath the Great Pyramid of Giza and it is that which is responsible for keeping mankind imprisoned in the two strands of DNA. I had also mentioned the possibility that amongst other reasons the Great Pyramid of Giza was also built to lead mankind astray. One is concentrating so heavily on why they were built but in the meantime forgets that there is much more there that needs to be researched. In my opinion Thoth was completely successful 16,000 years ago in placing future mankind in front of a mystery, a mystery which can only be solved when the time is right. It felt strange then when I decoded the number 84 as 'give up a mystery'. In my opinion the fact that this message can be found in a crop circle, which from the sky looks like a few pyramids, is not coincidental. 'In the past a mystery has been given which has more to it than meets the eye'. A somewhat remarkable message but I believe that it hits the nail right on the head.

I sometimes come across very extraordinary things during my quest to decipher the crop circle phenomenon. Previously I have described the white substance, which I had found in a crop circle formation and how the effects of it were tested on my being. During the testing we did end up discussing what I did in my daily life. I told Hellen that I was busy writing a book and during the conversation she shared with me the fact that through her guide she had received a 'message'. The message had said that the Great Pyramid had been built as an acupuncture point for the Earth to take care that mankind will receive the proper cosmic influence that it will need'. My first reaction was 'what?' and I even thought, ' yeah, right!' I am not someone who is known for believing everything that I hear but then I don't dismiss everything odd as an impossibility either.

Much later, after I had almost forgotten Hellen's pronouncement I came across an article with the heading 'Secret Numbers'. I thought 'hmmm, that could be interesting' and started reading the article especially because when you are occupied daily with crop circles and numbers a heading like that certainly catches your eye and every article relating to that subject matter is very interesting to me. Likewise with an article that appeared in January of 1999 in a Dutch magazine. The writer of the article 'Secret Numbers' tells us about the 'coincidence' that the Moon revolves around the Earth in 27.32 days. In that same time period the Moon turns a complete circle on it's own axis so that we always see the same side of the Moon. The absolute zero point is 273.2 °C. Again we see the same number only the decimal point has been moved over. This article tells us how the writer discovered many 'secret things'. For my feeling the most interesting part is the following.

The Earth does not stand up straight, but with regard to the Sun it's actually at a bit of an angle. This angle is called an inclination and amounts to 23.5°. The imaginary circle that the inclined Earth's axis traces in the heavens amounts to 25,920 years. After that extended period of time the axis 'points' to the same spot in the heavens as it did 25,920 years ago. The ancient Sumerians were already aware of this fact thousands of years ago.

The author of the article 'Secret Numbers' tells is that our body harbours the same numbers. Our heart is located at an angle compared to the line of our body. The angle of the heart amounts to the exact amount as the imaginary circle of precession that the Earth's axle is out of plumb, namely 23.5°. Coincidence? I don't think so. The article continues with the fact that a human has an average of 72 heartbeats per minute. Exactly, 72 can be converted to 9 and 72 is a Gematrian Number and it is 1 degree of the precession cycle. Man breathes an average of 18 breaths per minute (18 = 9). If you multiply the average of 18 breaths times 60 minutes times 24 hours then you have an average of 25,920 breaths every 24 hours. Was this not the same number as the precession cycle of the Earth? If you would apply the same calculations to the average heartbeat then you would get a result of 103,6880 (= 4 x 25,920).

What does this have to do with the Great Pyramid? If the Great Pyramid was built as a type of acupuncture point for the Earth to take care that mankind could receive the correct cosmic influence that they needed then it would be exactly right because as I mentioned before the Earth did not know of a precession cycle and the Earth stood upright before the great flood.

In Albert Slosman's book 'the astrology of ancient Egypt' he already described that according to the literal translations of the Egyptian hieroglyphics it said that 'the planets and permanent stars beneath the Big 9 (the Milky Way) navigated on according to the unfaltering ritual executed by the law of creation'. The seven planets from our solar system did not budge an inch from their path since the great disaster that turned the Earth's axis 180 degrees and also away from the Sun, in our field of vision, which stood at the head of the row of planets. The heavenly map of the temple of Dendera reinforces the exact stance of the stars as they stood on July

9792 (= 27/9) BC!Is it odd then to state that the Great Pyramid has been placed as a sort of acupuncture point? Is it also incredible to suggest that the builder of the Great Pyramid knew the future? Did he know when he would place the Great Pyramid exactly there where we still admire it today that it would be used as a sort of acupuncture pressure point? The same effect is accomplished when you take a small ball of styrofoam and put a pin in it. With a magnet you can then proceed to manipulate the ball any which way you choose. Is it strange to suppose that when the Earth's axle stood up straight and the Earth hung upside down that mankind did not have the correct cosmic influence at their disposal because the number of breaths and the position of the heart did not coincide with the numbers of the Earth?

To cut a long story short you could say that in this incomplete translation it says, ' in the past a mystery has been given which has much more to it then meets the eye'. Considering that I do not have access to the exact data of this formation I do not dare to firmly state with confidence what the translation ' the month July/August' and 'coming' could be referring to. The only thing that I can conclude from previous information and statistics is that the most crop circles 'come' into the fields in the months of 'July/August'.

The number 216

Of all the numbers that I have come across during the process of writing this book there is one combination in particular that has stayed with me all along. This is the number 216. From the first moment I saw this number I had a feeling that this number was important. I knew I recognised this number but I wasn't sure from where? I had come across it before, actually much earlier on in my life already. At a certain moment, and as you probably know these are very inconvenient moments when you have no pen or paper and it's the middle of the night, it rang a bell! It was the registration number of my military passport. In 1981 I had to report to the military, for what was then still a mandatory thing, to carry out the noble act of compulsory military service. I never stopped to think twice then, but as it seems now I was already 'connected/or better yet joined to the number 216. The registration in my passport consisted of my birthday written in reverse. What that means is that the year, month and date of birth are written and then the next number was 216. This number continued to intrigue me throughout my research. I came across this number everywhere. The number could be found in the inscription as well as the DNA formation. The Kings chamber of the Great Pyramid of Giza conceals this number. The beautiful yearly play of shadow on the Pyramid of Quetzalcoatl in Teotihuacan takes 66.6 seconds and 6 x 6 x 6 = 216.

Plato told us of the following about this particular number; 'that which is of godly origin has a circumference that is contained within a perfect number'. This number is calculated as 216. In my opinion the Bible also harbours this number in Revelations 13 vs18; ' This calls for wisdom. If anyone has insight, let him calculate the number of the beast, for it is man's number. His number is 666'. This number 666 is the same as 216 because 216 is built up out of 6 x 6 x 6 = 216. The question arises here as to why this number recurs in everything and what is the vibration of this number? If we were to know the vibration of this number then what could we do with it? In my opinion this number definitely has more than one meaning. One of the meanings that this number harbours within it is the following:

During the decoding of the crop circles covered by myself I also started on the Gematrian Numbers. I had a suspicion that there was more to it than just numbers. The number I started with was the number 36. The translation of this number is 'there is more to it'. Just as 216, 36 can be converted to 9. I write this as 216/9. The translation of this is 'signal' but if we reverse this as 9/216 then the translation is completely different and then it says 'in the future they will be coming!' A very remarkable result considering all the ancient civilisations talk about gods who will return again at some point.

Why England?

For the rest there remains one question, which keeps many of us occupied and that is; 'Why are most of the world wide occurring crop circles found in England?' I think I know the answer to that. The answer to this intriguing question is simple. It is the key to the solution of the mysterious crop circle phenomenon. In England the crop circle formations are measured with the duodecimal (12) standard unit of measurement. A system, which can be dated back to its original 60 number system (5 x 12 = 60) in ancient Sumeria by which one kept their trade contacts. With this we have ended back up in ancient Sumeria - the land of the gods. These are gods who were responsible for the previously mentioned enigmatic constructions that are thousands of years old. These gods have become active once again but only now they are active in world-wide grain fields to create the crop circle formations in them to clearly tell us what it is that has happened in the past. These are events that could possibly happen in the nearby future because history does repeat itself. Hopefully we will learn from the messages that can be found in the crop circles so that we will not make the same mistakes in the future as the ones we have made in the past.

Conclusion

After more than two years of research, investigations and lots of thought I have come to the conclusion that the world wide occurring crop circles are a derivative that originate from one or more groups of crop circle makers each with their own unique code or belonging to one group with a code consisting of different parts. Personally I think there is only one group of makers. A group that makes crop circles nowadays to tell mankind what has happened in the past. In my opinion it won't take very long before we get the messages that refer to the future and inform us as to what lies waiting for us. But to be able to understand everything we need to start at the beginning. We need to go back to the beginning years of the crop circle phenomenon to see what these, what appeared as simple formations, contain as far as hidden information is concerned. Only then will we be able to continue on step by step with our decoding of the crop circle formations. In my opinion when we have attained the level that we can read the mysterious phenomenon well then it won't be very long before we will find crop circles regarding our future.

According to my findings, the one group that is responsible for the making of the crop circles is the same as the one that was responsible for the construction of, amongst other things, the Pyramid complex of Giza, Teotihuacan, Angkor Wat, Stonehenge and so on. The same group that was responsible for the secret Gematrian numbers. These numbers can be found again in the crop circles. As a matter of fact the whole world is swarming with these numbers.

Pythagoras left us with the legacy of this passage; 'The Number is Everything'. 'Everything' such as colour, distance, messages and vibrations can be expressed by a number. The last one noted being especially important because 'everything' is vibration. 'Everything is Vibration, and Vibration is Everything'.

Epilogue

December 8, 1998. Two astronauts from the American space shuttle Endeavour have made the coupling between Zarya and the Unity, two parts of the yet to be built ISS, the International Space Station. There will be approximately 45 more flights into space before the space station can be ready in 2004.

Is this purely coincidental that there is an International space station being built or is there more to it? Most likely the leaders of this common project will never share this with the average citizen yet it is peculiar that it is happening in these times of changes. Coincidence? Maybe it has to do with the approaching of the planet Nibiru? Is one expecting the arrival of the planet when it is halfway through its revolution or is it that the planet is actually closer to our Solar System then we think. Does one simply want to be informed as soon as possible of the arrival of our 'creators' or does one want to stop them dead in their tracks, make them fall out of the sky and proceed to tell mankind that they had evil intentions. This could be done so that man could continue to live peacefully on Earth, never knowing any better and never being told the truth.

Is it possible that there is also more known about the world-wide occurring phenomenon of crop circle formations and the possibility of messages that are present in the formations? Are the Americans really in possession of extraterrestrial technology just as the rumours say? Why did the Vatican never bring out the message of Fatima into the open? Is mankind not ready for such a message as it was told? Or is it not being told because otherwise one would lose ' the power over the ordinary people'.

Quite often the beginning of the world is described as a total void. Many old myths and legends talk about the universe as a cosmic egg that has all the potentials concealed within it. Furthermore all the ancient civilisations talk about the coming and going of the gods. Even the great flood is an occurrence that is talked about in all the

Crop Circles, Gods and their Secrets

stories just as the promise that the gods will return sometime is. Are all the myths nonsense? Were all the ancient civilisations stark raving mad? Did they only write down all this nonsense to leave us this legacy of a fun puzzle? Were these prehistoric authors with their science fiction stories ahead of their time? Is there truth in all the myths and legends? Shouldn't we start looking at all these stories through a pair of 'symbolic glasses'. Are all the ancient traditions showing us the actual facts of history? Are most of the scientific scholars knowingly blinkered about this information or does it purely not fit into their narrow 'regular' street and is it simply being ignored? Is one afraid to completely research all these statistics because they are afraid that the outcome will show us everything did indeed go differently and then what has been given as a false hope of prediction for all these years would be proven wrong? Are people like Erich vön Däniken and Zecharia Sitchin not crazy as is presumed but perhaps have been right all along.

If this is the case I can just imagine that a lot of effort is being put into keeping mankind ignorant of any of these facts today. If things have really gone as the legends and myths have been telling us and having us believe then it is about time that we scratch ourselves behind the ears and start revising our history. Do the things that we are told tally up? Are our 'creators' really beings from another planet? Are we to be thankful to the 'extra-terrestrials' for everything? Are they the ones who are writing their names and symbols in the grain as we have seen in the inscription and the DNA formation close to Alton Barnes? Are the world-wide occurring crop circle formations an attempt from the 'gods' to warn us about the inevitable that is coming? That way there is no one, who can avoid the issue, everyone can see these symbols in the grain fields. Did they really depart centuries ago as the ancient writings tell us or did they simply stay amongst us in another dimension? A dimension that we cannot perceive yet with our naked (earthly) eyes?

Many questions will remain unanswered forever and undoubtedly many questions will be added to the list but still in my eyes there are just too many 'coincidences'. We could certainly keep up this farce and dismiss all the facts onto the 'land of fairy tales' but if we really want to know the truth we need to look within because all things considered the truth lies within ourselves.

But as usual, time will tell.

Robert Boerman, Brummen, the Netherlands, 2003

Questions

For more information about Dutch crop circles from 1590 until the present, interested readers can go to the Dutch Crop Circle Archive, the website of the PTAH Foundation at: www.dcca.nl. For further questions, one can reach me via info@dcca.nl

Photo credits

Thanks must go to those listed below for photographic illustrations and copyrighted images:

P 22   - Zierikzee, July 17, 1997 © Joop van Houdt
P 31   - © Stichting Wakker Dier
P 33   - Above: Zierikzee, July 17, 1997 © Joop van Houdt
         Below: Windmill Hill, August 2, 1996 © Janet Ossebaard
P 36/42 - All illustrations © Bert Janssen
P 48   - Dead Flies © Janet Ossebaard
P 56   - Milk Hill, Wiltshire, 1991 © Andrew King
P 66   - East Field, Alton Barnes, Wiltshire, June 17, 1996
            © Lucy Pringle
P 69   - Milk Hill, Wiltshire, 1991 © Andrew King
P 85/91 - Pyramids of Giza © Marianna Ringelberg
P 98   - Allington Down, July 16, 1999 © Janet Ossebaard
P 103   - Missing Earth, Winchester, Hampshire, June 25, 1995
            © Janet Ossebaard
P 113   - East Field, Alton Barnes, Wiltshire, June 17, 1996
            © Lucy Pringle
P 147   - Windmill Hill, Wiltshire, July 16, 1999 © Janet Ossebaard
P 155   - Devils Den, Wiltshire, July 20, 2001 © Janet Ossebaard

All other photographs and illustrations © Robert Boerman.

While every effort has been made to secure permissions, if there are any errors or oversights regarding copyright material, the author will be pleased to rectify these at the earliest opportunity and to give appropriate acknowledgement in any future edition.

Bibliography

Erfenis der Goden - Andrew Collins - Bosch en Keuning - ISBN 90-246-0441-9

Kosmische slinger der tijden - Wim Zitman - De ring - ISBN 90-74358-04-7

Graancirkels, codes uit een andere dimensie - Rudi Klijnstra - Ankh Hermes -ISBN 90-202-8118-6

Andere Dimensies, voor bij tijd en ruimte - Rudi Klijnstra - Petiet - ISBN 90-75636-17-2

Het raadsel van de graancirkels - Eltjo H. Haselhoff - Ankh Hermes - ISBN 90-202-8162-3

Boodschappen uit de kosmos - Michael Hesemann/Herman Hegge - Tirion - ISBN 90-5121-546-0

Wat wisten de Maya's ? - Peter Toonen - Petiet - ISBN 90-75636-14-8

Leylijnen en Leycentra in de Lage Landen - Wigholt Vleer - Ankh Hermes - ISBN 90-2002-1099

Het ontstaan en het einde van alles - Graham Hancock - Tirion - ISBN 90-5121-600-9

The 12th Planet - Zecharia Sitchin - Avon Books - ISBN 0-380-39362-X

When time began - Zecharia Sitchin - Avon Books - ISBN 0-389-77071-7

The lost realms - Zecharia Sitchin - Avon Books - ISBN 0-380-

75890-3

Gods of the new millennium - Alan Alford - Hodder & Stoughton Ltd. London - 1997

Edgar Cayce over Atlantis - Edgar Evans Cayce - De Ster - ISBN 90-6556-061-0

Sefer Yetzirah - Aryeh Kaplan - Samuel Weiser - ISBN 0-87728-855-0

Mysteries of the Mexican Piramids - Peter Tomkins - Harper and Row - ISBN 0-06-091-366-5

Mythen van de Mensheid - Roy Willis - Anthos - ISBN 90-6074-914-6

Mythen en legenden - Arthur Cotterell - Atrium - ISBN 90-6113-819-1

Zonnegoden en Offerdoden - Diverse schrijvers - Time Life Books - ISBN 90-5390-204-X

Flower of Life - Drunvalo Melchizedek - by Val Valerian - ISBN 9990-184789

In de schaduw van de Piramiden - Erich von Däniken - Luitingh-Sijthof - ISBN 90-245-260-9

Het Aliën logboek - Jim Marrs - Tirion - ISBN 90-5121-750-1

De Bijbelcode - Michael Drosnin - Strengholt - ISBN - 90 6010 935 x

De geweide aarde - Brian Leigh Molyneaux - ISBN 90 215 2675 1 - Kosmos-Z&K

Kabbalah - Charles Ponce - ISBN - 90-202-4840-5

Popul Vuh - Wolfgang Cordan - Ankh-Hermes - ISBN 90 202 4856 1
Astrologie van het oude Egypte - Albert Slosman - Mirananda - ISBN
90 6271 734 9

Toetanchamon - Thomas Hoving - Helmond - ISBN 90 252 6964 8

DARWIN'S MISTAKE
Dr Hans Zillmer

Yes, there were cataclysms (among them The Flood) in the course of history, but no, there was no evolution. The Earth's crust is relatively young and no more than a few thousand years ago; its poles were free of ice.
Published in nine languages, this international bestseller puts the latest discoveries and new evidence against Darwin's Theory of Evolution. The author, who owes his insights and expertise to numerous excavations he participated in, describes recent findings that – in line with suppressed results of scientific research – prove what seems unthinkable to us today: Darwin was wrong.

120 Pages. Paperback. Euro 25,90 * GBP 14.99 * USD $ 19.95. Code: DMIS

SAUNIERE'S MODEL AND THE SECRET OF RENNES-LE-CHATEAU

André Douzet

After years of research, André Douzet discovered a model ordered by abbé Bérenger Saunière. Douzet reveals that Saunière spent large amounts of time and money in the city of Lyons... trips he went on in the utmost secrecy. Douzet finally unveils the location indicated on the model, the location of Saunière's secret.

116 Pages. Paperback. Euro 14,90 * GBP 7.99 * USD $ 12.00. Code: SMOD

THE TEMPLARS' LEGACY IN MONTREAL, THE NEW JERUSALEM

Francine Bernier

Montréal, Canada. Designed in the 17th Century as the New Jerusalem of the Christian world, the island of Montreal became the new headquarters of a group of mystics that wanted to live as the flawless Primitive Church of Jesus. But why could they not do that in the Old World? The people behind the scene in turning this dream into reality were the *Société de Notre-Dame*, half of whose members were in the elusive Compagnie du Saint-Sacrement. Like their Templar predecessors, they worked for humanity. Montréal's destiny was to become the refuge of the most virtuous men and women who expected the return of a divine king-priest; a story connected with the revival of a heterodox group whose marks, and those of the French masonic Compagnons, are still visible today, both in the old Montréal city… and underneath.
*360 pages. Paperback. GBP 14.99 * USD $21.95 * Euro 25.00. code: TLIM*

NOSTRADAMUS AND THE LOST TEMPLAR LEGACY

Rudy Cambier

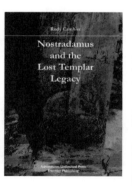

Nostradamus' Prophecies were *not* written in ca. 1550 by the French "visionary" Michel de Nostradame. Instead, they were composed between 1323 and 1328 by a Cistercian monk, Yves de Lessines, prior of the Cistercian abbey of Cambron, on the border between France and Belgium. They reveal the location of a Templar treasure. Nostradamus' "prophecies" has shown that the language of those verses does not belong in the 16th Century, nor in Nostradamus' region. The language spoken in the verses belongs to the medieval times of the 14th Century, and the Belgian borders, not the French Provence in the 16th Century. " The location identified in the documents has since been shown to indeed contain what Yves de Lessines said they would contain: barrels with gold, silver and documents.
*192 pages. Paperback. USD $ 17,95 * GBP 11,99 * Euro 22.90. code: NLTL*

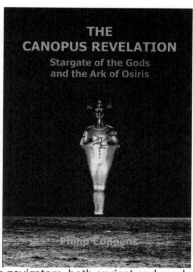